THE SURVEY OF ACADEMIC LIBRARIES, 2006-07 EDITION

ISBN#: 1-57440-080-0   © 2006 Primary Research Group, Inc.

12-06   #71963968

18

SUMMARY OF MAIN FINDINGS

- Mean library staff for the colleges in the sample was about 18.31 and ranged from one to 120. Community college staffs averaged 4.44 while colleges offering PHD's averaged library staff of more than 32.

- A mean of about 42.4% of the total library staff had MLS degrees, an average of 7.76 librarians with MLS degrees per survey participant.

- The mean annual cost of compensation for the libraries in the sample was $669,911, a modest 2.1% increase over the 2005 figure of $655,758.

- A shade more than 34% of the libraries in the sample felt that in the past year compensation for librarians on staff had declined in real terms.

- The libraries in the sample spent a mean of only $2,863 for degrees or continuing education for library staff, a surprising finding, given all the publicity given to the potential shortage of librarians.

- Hiring plans for new librarians was relatively strong with total demand per library at a respectable 0.67 new librarians.   However, no community college in the sample planned to hire a librarian in the next year.

- The libraries in the sample spent a mean of about 159.3 hours per year of staff time addressing problems related to the interruption of database access, or about 4 solid weeks of full time work.

- Mean spending on library materials/content for the libraries in the sample was approximately $404,465 in 2006, an increase of 11.4% over 2005 mean spending of $362,970.

- The libraries in the sample tried a mean of 5.68 databases on a free trial basis in the past year and subsequently acquired paid access to a mean of 2.08 of these databases.

- Mean spending on electronic databases for content was approximately $164,732 in 2006, up significantly from $144,447 in 2005, a one year increase of 14%. This figure covers all electronic databases, including those on tape and cd-rom, as well as web or other online delivered databases.

- The largest libraries in terms of enrollment base served were much more likely to cite "Publisher Claims of Non-Payment" as a reason for database access interruption.

- Many colleges still have problems with failures of their own computer networks as a reason for interruptions in database access. Community colleges in particular cited this as a reason for database access interruption.

- The mean value of spending derived from grants for the libraries in the sample was $50,055 in 2006. Most libraries in the sample had no grant income but a substantial minority did. Note that in 2005 total value of grant spending by the libraries in the sample was less than $13,000 so this figure is volatile and can be shifted by a few large grant recipients.

- The libraries in the sample spent a mean of only 59.55 hours in staff time annually in preparing grants for the library; the median was only 22.5 hours.

- The mean number of grants applied for in the past year was only 1.5.

- The libraries in the sample accrued a mean of only $12,166 from special endowments in the past year, with a median of $2,500.

- About 27% of the libraries in the sample had special endowments targeted at book collections, while only 9.62% had special endowments targeted at electronic assets.

- Subscriptions obtained through consortiums account for a mean of 67% and a median of 75% of the database subscriptions of the libraries in the sample. Community colleges went directly to publishers more often than other types of colleges: consortium purchases accounted for a bit less than 58% of their database subscriptions.

- Most libraries pay their subscription agents in a lump sum at the beginning of the year, but a small minority, a bit less than 13%, pay their agents in increments throughout the year.

- About 79% of periodicals spending by the libraries in the sample is accounted for by spending through subscription agents.

- More than 40% of the libraries in the sample have a center or specific set of workstations earmarked for computer or information literacy of some kind.

- Mean spending on electronic books has increased substantially over the past three years, rising from a library mean of $6,692 in 2005, to $7,370 in 2006, and an anticipated $8,706 in 2007.

- Spending on traditional books by the libraries in the sample increased by 6.6% in 2006, rising from a mean of $76,045 to $81,079.

- The libraries in the sample purchased a mean of 79.1% of their books through book distributors or jobbers. Libraries from PHD granting institutions actually acquired a lower percentage of their total books through book jobbers or distributors than other types of libraries, perhaps reflecting their more eclectic and diverse needs.

- About 34.9% of the libraries in the sample have lap top lending programs to students. Of those that do not currently have such a program, only 3.85% say that they have firm plans to start one within the next two years, but close to 20% say that they might possibly start such a program within this time frame.

- Spending on journals in both print and electronic formats was a mean of $214,507 in 2005, and rose to $227,800, an increase of 6.2%, a relatively low increase by historic standards, but high relative to other mediums. The libraries in the sample expected to increase mean spending to $239,294 in 2007, an increase of 5.05%, once again, low by historic standards for this medium.

- Only 2.44% of the libraries in the sample maintained a digital depository for works by their own faculty members and all were PHD-granting institutions. A bit more than 10% of the colleges in the sample plan to develop a digital depository within the next two years and a further third say that it is a possibility.

- Almost 37% of the libraries in the sample spend about 10% of total librarian staff time conducting classes, seminars and formal tutorials for students and faculty. A lightly lower percentage – 34.15% -- spend between 10% and 20% of their staff time on these pursuits. Nearly a quarter of the libraries in the sample spend between 20% and 35% of librarians staff time in teaching, while 4.88% spend from 35% to 50% of their time doing so.

- More than 71% of the libraries in the sample said that their student education work load had increased over the past two years, while less than 5% said that this work load had declined in this period.

- The librarians in the sample spent a mean of 8.89% of their total staff time in responding to queries from patrons located outside the library about use of the library's databases.

- 34% of the libraries in the sample maintain a rare books collection.

- The colleges in the sample spent a mean of $7,491 on audio visual materials in 2005, and increased spending significantly to $8,222 in 2006. Also, colleges expected to significantly increase spending once again in 2007, to a mean of $8,908.

- More than half of the libraries in the sample now catalog web resources, and even more than 57% of community colleges do so. Close to 32% of the libraries in the sample make archival and finding aids available on the web.

- The college libraries in the sample spent a mean of $20,493 on their cataloging department budget, or its equivalent, if they had no such department

DIMENSIONS OF THE SAMPLE

Mean, Median, Minimum and Maximum College Enrollment

	Mean	Median	Minimum	Maximum
All Libraries	3925.98	2400.00	100.00	20000.00

Mean, Median, Minimum and Maximum College Enrollment, Broken Out by College Enrollment Category

	Mean	Median	Minimum	Maximum
Less than 1,650	1081.10	1225.00	100.00	1650.00
1650 -- 4,000	2822.53	2747.00	1800.00	3750.00
Greater than 4,000	9964.54	8355.00	4200.00	20000.00

Mean, Median, Minimum and Maximum College Enrollment, Broken Out by Type of College

Type of College	Mean	Median	Minimum	Maximum
Community College	2066.33	1100.00	500.00	7500.00
4 Year or Masters Level	3020.96	1800.00	600.00	20000.00
PHD or Research University Level	6865.53	3700.00	500.00	20000.00

Mean, Median, Minimum and Maximum College Enrollment, Broken Out by Public or Private Status of the College

	Mean	Median	Minimum	Maximum
Public College	6755.95	4532.50	500.00	20000.00
Private College	2100.19	1650.00	100.00	8355.00

Enrollment figures are full time equivalent

1. CHAPTER ONE: LIBRARY STAFFING BENCHMARKS

Mean library staff for the colleges in the sample was about 18.31, and ranged from one to 120. Community college staffs averaged 4.44 while colleges offering PHD's averaged library staff of more than 32.

About 42.4% of the total staff, on average, had MLS degrees. This ratio was slightly higher for 4-year and MA granting institutions than it was for community colleges. For BA and MA granting institutions, employees with MLS degrees accounted for 46.93% of employees, while on the community college library staffs, the percentage was 42.34% and for PHD and research level institutions, only 38.33% of staff had MLS degrees, perhaps reflecting greater use of library technicians among these institutions. The mean and median number of MLS trained librarians employed by the libraries in the sample were very close, suggesting only relatively modest levels of variance. Most colleges tended to keep the percentage of MLS trained librarians at less than half of their total library staff.

Employment of library technicians rose significantly with library size. Libraries from colleges with more than 4,000 students employed more than 3x as many library technicians as those with from 1,650 to 4,000 students.

1.1. Mean, Median, Minimum and Maximum Library Staff

	Mean	Median	Minimum	Maximum
All Libraries	18.31	10.75	1.00	120.00

1.2. Mean, Median, Minimum and Maximum Library Staff, Broken Out by College Enrollment

Number of Enrolled Students (FTE)	Mean	Median	Minimum	Maximum
Less than 1,650	7.12	7.50	1.00	18.00
1650 -- 4,000	13.07	13.50	6.00	24.00
Greater than 4,000	47.43	44.75	7.00	120.00

1.3. Mean, Median, Minimum and Maximum Library Staff, Broken Out by Type of College

Type of College	Mean	Median	Minimum	Maximum
Community College	4.44	3.75	1.00	10.50
4-Year or Master's Level	14.43	10.00	3.75	69.00
PHD & Research University	32.32	17.00	6.00	120.00

1.4. Mean, Median, Minimum and Maximum Library Staff, Broken Out by Public or Private Status of the College

Public or Private Status	Mean	Median	Minimum	Maximum
Public College	29.06	16.12	1.00	120.00
Private College	12.16	8.80	1.00	72.00

1.5. Mean, Median, Minimum and Maximum Number of Librarians with an MLS Degree Employed by the Library

	Mean	Median	Minimum	Maximum
All Libraries	7.76	5.25	1.00	35.00

1.6. Mean, Median, Minimum and Maximum Number of Librarians with an MLS Degree Employed by the Library, Broken Out by College Enrollment

Number of Enrolled Students (FTE)	Mean	Median	Minimum	Maximum
Less than 1,650	3.61	3.00	1.00	8.00
1650 -- 4,000	5.90	5.00	1.00	11.00
Greater than 4,000	18.45	16.75	7.00	35.00

1.7. Mean, Median, Minimum and Maximum Number of Librarians with an MLS Degree Employed by the Library, Broken Out by Type of College

Type of College	Mean	Median	Minimum	Maximum
Community College	1.88	1.00	1.00	5.00
4-Year or Master's Level	6.96	5.75	2.00	30.00
PHD & Research University	12.39	7.75	4.00	35.00

1.8. Mean, Median, Minimum and Maximum Number of Librarians with an MLS Degree Employed by the Library, Broken Out by Public or Private Status of the College

Public or Private Status	Mean	Median	Minimum	Maximum
Public College	11.34	8.50	1.00	35.00
Private College	5.72	4.80	1.00	28.00

1.9. Mean, Median, Minimum and Maximum Number of Library Assistants or Technicians, 2005, Employed by the Library

	Mean	Median	Minimum	Maximum
All Libraries	9.03	5.50	0.00	65.00

1.10. Mean, Median, Minimum and Maximum Number of Library Assistants or Technicians, 2005, Employed by the Library, Broken Out by College Enrollment

Number of Enrolled Students (FTE)	Mean	Median	Minimum	Maximum
Less than 1,650	3.45	3.00	0.00	12.00
1650 -- 4,000	6.80	6.50	2.00	13.00
Greater than 4,000	22.98	19.90	6.00	65.00

1.11. Mean, Median, Minimum and Maximum Number of Library Assistants or Technicians, 2005, Employed by the Library, Broken Out by Type of College

Type of College	Mean	Median	Minimum	Maximum
Community College	2.06	1.50	0.00	7.50
4-Year or Master's Level	6.32	5.00	1.00	15.00
PHD & Research University	17.27	9.50	2.00	65.00

1.12. Mean, Median, Minimum and Maximum Number of Library Assistants or Technicians, 2005, Employed by the Library, Broken Out by Public or Private Status of the College

Public or Private Status	Mean	Median	Minimum	Maximum
Public College	14.72	8.75	1.00	65.00
Private College	5.78	4.00	0.00	24.80

The mean annual cost of compensation for the libraries in the sample was $669,911; annual compensation costs for the community colleges in the sample was $133,315, less than a fifth of the costs for 4-year or Master's level institutions, which spent a mean of $692,255 on annual compensation for the library staff.

1.13. Mean, Median, Minimum and Maximum Annual Cost of Salaries, Benefits and other Compensation, 2006 (in $)

	Mean	Median	Minimum	Maximum
All Libraries	669911.03	340000.00	50000.00	2750000.00

1.14. Mean, Median, Minimum and Maximum Annual Cost of Salaries, Benefits and other Compensation (in $), Broken Out by College Enrollment

Number of Enrolled Students (FTE)	Mean	Median	Minimum	Maximum
Less than 1,650	277623.33	280510.00	50000.00	965000.00
1650 -- 4,000	567885.08	544148.00	82136.00	1381690.00
Greater than 4,000	1558489.38	1566550.50	297000.00	2750000.00

1.15. Mean, Median, Minimum and Maximum Annual Cost of Salaries, Benefits and other Compensation (in $), Broken Out by Type of College

Type of College	Mean	Median	Minimum	Maximum
Community College	133315.40	116000.00	50000.00	239447.00
4-Year or Master's Level	629687.16	363132.00	82136.00	2438964.00
PHD & Research University	983295.73	566237.00	254000.00	2750000.00

1.16. Mean, Median, Minimum and Maximum Annual Cost of Salaries, Benefits and other Compensation (in $), Broken Out by Public or Private Status of the College

Public or Private Status	Mean	Median	Minimum	Maximum
Public College	1111849.20	857500.00	196130.00	2438964.00
Private College	493135.76	315000.00	50000.00	2750000.00

1.17. Mean, Median, Minimum and Maximum Annual Cost of Salaries, Benefits and other Compensation, 2005 (in $)

	Mean	Median	Minimum	Maximum
All Libraries	655757.97	381788.00	47000.00	2637782.00

1.18. Mean, Median, Minimum and Maximum Annual Cost of Salaries, Benefits and other Compensation, 2005 (in $), Broken Out by College Enrollment

Number of Enrolled Students (FTE)	Mean	Median	Minimum	Maximum
Less than 1,650	275180.13	252893.00	47000.00	948500.00
1650 -- 4,000	589840.67	545549.50	209892.00	1207904.00
Greater than 4,000	1468217.38	1355515.00	315000.00	2637782.00

1.19. Mean, Median, Minimum and Maximum Annual Cost of Salaries, Benefits and other Compensation, 2005 (in $), Broken Out by Type of College

Type of College	Mean	Median	Minimum	Maximum
Community College	125415.20	110000.00	47000.00	209892.00
4-Year or Master's Level	646131.95	465000.00	105039.00	2355000.00
PHD & Research University	913449.64	545106.00	223500.00	2637782.00

1.20. Mean, Median, Minimum and Maximum Annual Cost of Salaries, Benefits and other Compensation, 2005 (in $), Broken Out by Public or Private Status of the College

Public or Private Status	Mean	Median	Minimum	Maximum
Public College	1046153.30	849250.00	195184.00	2355000.00
Private College	499599.84	305000.00	47000.00	2637782.00

PHD-level and research universities employed most of the subject specialist librarians in the sample. Most community colleges did not employ a subject specialist, and mean employment of subject specialists for them was less than 0.5. Even 4-year and Master's granting institutions employed only a mean of 2.10 subject specialist librarians and most did not employ any at all. The PHD and research level universities in the sample employed a mean of more than 8 subject specialist librarians.

1.21. Mean, Median, Minimum and Maximum Number of Subject Specialists Librarians Employed by the Library

	Mean	Median	Minimum	Maximum
All Libraries	2.54	0.00	0.00	25.00

1.22. Mean, Median, Minimum and Maximum Number of Subject Specialists Librarians Employed by the Library, Broken Out by College Enrollment

Number of Enrolled Students (FTE)	Mean	Median	Minimum	Maximum
Less than 1,650	0.47	0.00	0.00	3.00
1650 -- 4,000	1.25	0.00	0.00	10.00
Greater than 4,000	8.10	0.00	0.00	25.00

1.23. Mean, Median, Minimum and Maximum Number of Subject Specialists Librarians Employed by the Library, Broken Out by Type of College

Type of College	Mean	Median	Minimum	Maximum
Community College	0.33	0.00	0.00	1.00
4-Year or Master's Level	2.10	0.00	0.00	22.00
PHD & Research University	4.32	0.00	0.00	25.00

1.24. Mean, Median, Minimum and Maximum Number of Subject Specialists Librarians Employed by the Library, Broken Out by Public or Private Status of the College

Public or Private Status	Mean	Median	Minimum	Maximum
Public College	4.64	0.00	0.00	25.00
Private College	1.54	0.00	0.00	17.00

A shade more than 34% of the libraries in the sample felt that in the past year compensation for librarians had declined in real terms. Interestingly enough, a full 70% of libraries in colleges with more than 4,000 students felt that library compensation had declined in real terms within the past year, as did nearly 43% of PHD and research level universities. Only 12.5% of community college librarians felt that their compensation had declined in real terms within the past year.

1.25. Trend in Compensation Growth

	More or less declined in real terms	Kept up with inflation	Increased in real terms by a few percent	Increased in real terms by more than 5 percent
All Libraries	34.09%	40.91%	22.73%	2.27%

1.26. Trend in Compensation Growth, Broken Out by College Enrollment

Number of Enrolled Students (FTE)	More or less declined in real terms	Kept up with inflation	Increased in real terms by a few percent	Increased in real terms by more than 5 percent
Less than 1,650	26.32%	47.37%	26.32%	0.00%
1650 -- 4,000	20.00%	53.33%	26.67%	0.00%
Greater than 4,000	70.00%	10.00%	10.00%	10.00%

1.27. Trend in Compensation Growth, Broken Out by Type of College

Type of College	More or less declined in real terms	Kept up with inflation	Increased in real terms by a few percent	Increased in real terms by more than 5 percent
Community College	12.50%	37.50%	50.00%	0.00%
4-Year or Master's Level	36.36%	40.91%	22.73%	0.00%
PHD & Research University	42.86%	42.86%	7.14%	7.14%

1.28. Trend in Compensation Growth, Broken Out by Public or Private Status of the College

Public or Private Status	More or less declined in real terms	Kept up with inflation	Increased in real terms by a few percent	Increased in real terms by more than 5 percent
Public College	43.75%	31.25%	18.75%	6.25%
Private College	28.57%	46.43%	25.00%	0.00%

The libraries in the sample spent a mean of only $2,863 for degrees or continuing education for library staff, a surprising finding, given all the publicity given to the potential shortage of librarians. If there is such a shortage, employers are not dealing with it by opening the purse strings for librarian education to "grow from within". Median spending was less than $800.00 per library, a sorry statistic. A handful of libraries appear to account for the bulk of spending. Academic librarians generally enjoy good benefits packages, but this is not a promising result.

Hiring plans for new librarians was relatively strong with total demand per library at a respectable 0.67 new librarians. No community college in the sample planned to hire a librarian in the next year.

1.29. Mean, Median, Minimum and Maximum Library Spending on Degrees or Continuing Education for Library Staff (in $)

	Mean	Median	Minimum	Maximum
All Libraries	2862.88	1000.00	0.00	25000.00

1.30. Mean, Median, Minimum and Maximum Library Spending on Degrees or Continuing Education for Library Staff (in $), Broken Out by College Enrollment

Number of Enrolled Students (FTE)	Mean	Median	Minimum	Maximum
Less than 1,650	1547.94	800.00	0.00	8000.00
1650 -- 4,000	4205.56	2297.50	0.00	21100.00
Greater than 4,000	3722.22	0.00	0.00	25000.00

1.31. Mean, Median, Minimum and Maximum Library Spending on Degrees or Continuing Education for Library Staff (in $), Broken Out by Type of College

Type of College	Mean	Median	Minimum	Maximum
Community College	785.71	200.00	0.00	2500.00
4-Year or Master's Level	2997.18	1000.00	0.00	21100.00
PHD & Research University	3984.62	2000.00	0.00	25000.00

1.32. Mean, Median, Minimum and Maximum Library Spending on Degrees or Continuing Education for Library Staff (in $), Broken Out by Public or Private Status of the College

Public or Private Status	Mean	Median	Minimum	Maximum
Public College	1500.00	0.00	0.00	6000.00
Private College	3675.59	1488.00	0.00	25000.00

1.33. Mean, Median, Minimum and Maximum Number of Librarians that the Library Plans to Hire in the Next Year

	Mean	Median	Minimum	Maximum
All Libraries	0.67	0.00	0.00	5.00

1.34. Mean, Median, Minimum and Maximum Number of Librarians that the Library Plans to Hire in the Next Year, Broken Out by College Enrollment

Number of Enrolled Students (FTE)	Mean	Median	Minimum	Maximum
Less than 1,650	0.28	0.00	0.00	1.00
1650 -- 4,000	0.71	1.00	0.00	2.00
Greater than 4,000	1.44	1.00	0.00	5.00

1.35. Mean, Median, Minimum and Maximum Number of Librarians that the Library Plans to Hire in the Next Year, Broken Out by Type of College

Type of College	Mean	Median	Minimum	Maximum
Community College	0.00	0.00	0.00	0.00
4-Year or Master's Level	0.55	0.50	0.00	2.00
PHD & Research University	1.23	1.00	0.00	5.00

1.36. Mean, Median, Minimum and Maximum Number of Librarians that the Library Plans to Hire in the Next Year, Broken Out by Public or Private Status of the College

Public or Private Status	Mean	Median	Minimum	Maximum
Public College	1.00	0.50	0.00	5.00
Private College	0.52	0.00	0.00	2.00

2. CHAPTER TWO: SPENDING ON CONTENT/MATERIALS

Mean spending on library materials/content for the libraries in the sample was approximately $404,465 in 2006, an increase of 11.4% over 2005 mean spending of $362,970.

2.1. Mean, Median, Minimum and Maximum Library Spending on Materials/Content in 2006 (in $)

	Mean	Median	Minimum	Maximum
All Libraries	404464.98	216315.50	18000.00	2700000.00

2.2. Mean, Median, Minimum and Maximum Library Spending on Materials/Content in 2006 (in $), Broken Out by College Enrollment

Number of Enrolled Students (FTE)	Mean	Median	Minimum	Maximum
Less than 1,650	129910.19	136885.00	18000.00	250000.00
1650 -- 4,000	386725.73	350000.00	59155.00	900000.00
Greater than 4,000	1029893.75	980918.00	200000.00	2700000.00

2.3. Mean, Median, Minimum and Maximum Library Spending on Materials/Content in 2006 (in $), Broken Out by Type of College

Type of College	Mean	Median	Minimum	Maximum
Community College	48072.50	49577.50	18000.00	77000.00
4-Year or Master's Level	368105.40	225200.00	82068.00	1300000.00
PHD & Research University	761082.82	498000.00	187000.00	2700000.00

2.4. Mean, Median, Minimum and Maximum Library Spending on Materials/Content in 2006 (in $), Broken Out by Public or Private Status of the College

Public or Private Status	Mean	Median	Minimum	Maximum
Public College	575601.08	250000.00	40000.00	2700000.00
Private College	332145.58	216315.50	18000.00	1321491.00

2.5. Mean, Median, Minimum and Maximum Library Spending on Materials/Content in the 2005 Academic Year (in $)

	Mean	Median	Minimum	Maximum
All Libraries	362970.30	207003.50	8300.00	2600000.00

2.6. Mean, Median, Minimum and Maximum Library Spending on Materials/Content in the 2005 Academic Year (in $), Broken Out by College Enrollment

Number of Enrolled Students (FTE)	Mean	Median	Minimum	Maximum
Less than 1,650	132200.56	142885.00	8300.00	250000.00
1650 -- 4,000	350111.87	226187.00	59155.00	900000.00
Greater than 4,000	890740.63	846418.00	200000.00	2600000.00

2.7. Mean, Median, Minimum and Maximum Library Spending on Materials/Content in the 2005 Academic Year (in $), Broken Out by Type of College

Type of College	Mean	Median	Minimum	Maximum
Community College	48624.71	59155.00	8300.00	84403.00
4-Year or Master's Level	324716.57	209007.00	60139.00	1031000.00
PHD & Research University	666671.91	389543.00	185352.00	2600000.00

2.8. Mean, Median, Minimum and Maximum Library Spending on Materials/Content in the 2005-06 Academic Year (in $), Broken Out by Public or Private Status of the College

Public or Private Status	Mean	Median	Minimum	Maximum
Public College	504951.92	200000.00	35000.00	2600000.00
Private College	304939.88	209220.50	8300.00	1099643.00

3. CHAPTER THREE: USE OF ELECTRONIC MATERIALS/CONTENT

Mean spending on electronic databases for content was approximately $164,732 in 2006, up significantly from $144,447 in 2005, a one year increase of 14%. This figure covers all electronic databases, including those on tape and cd-rom, as well as web or other online delivered databases.

3.1. Mean, Median, Minimum and Maximum Library Spending on Materials/Content in 2006 (in $)

	Mean	Median	Minimum	Maximum
All Libraries	164732.16	69679.00	6388.00	1300000.00

3.2. Mean, Median, Minimum and Maximum Library Spending on Materials/Content in 2006 (in $), Broken Out by College Enrollment

Number of Enrolled Students (FTE)	Mean	Median	Minimum	Maximum
Less than 1,650	85839.93	41250.00	6388.00	644000.00
1650 -- 4,000	107284.86	87344.00	26000.00	253306.00
Greater than 4,000	420542.88	225000.00	30000.00	1300000.00

3.3. Mean, Median, Minimum and Maximum Library Spending on Materials/Content in 2006 (in $), Broken Out by Type of College

Type of College	Mean	Median	Minimum	Maximum
Community College	19050.00	11662.00	6388.00	50000.00
4-Year or Master's Level	170384.83	78511.50	30000.00	860000.00
PHD & Research University	260710.27	109286.00	56660.00	1300000.00

3.4. Mean, Median, Minimum and Maximum Library Spending on Materials/Content in 2006 (in $), Broken Out by Public or Private Status of the College

Public or Private Status	Mean	Median	Minimum	Maximum
Public College	249397.92	45000.00	10000.00	1300000.00
Private College	128138.13	72646.50	6388.00	644000.00

3.5. Mean, Median, Minimum and Maximum Library Spending on Electronic Materials/Content in 2005 Academic Year (in $)

	Mean	Median	Minimum	Maximum
All Libraries	144447.27	52000.00	0.00	1100000.00

3.6. Mean, Median, Minimum and Maximum Library Spending on Electronic Materials/Content in 2005 (in $), Broken Out by College Enrollment

Number of Enrolled Students (FTE)	Mean	Median	Minimum	Maximum
Less than 1,650	64100.13	37000.00	4500.00	430000.00
1650 -- 4,000	92447.64	71168.00	20734.00	216240.00
Greater than 4,000	386097.50	254890.00	0.00	1100000.00

3.7. Mean, Median, Minimum and Maximum Library Spending on Electronic Materials/Content in 2005 (in $), Broken Out by Type of College

Type of College	Mean	Median	Minimum	Maximum
Community College	16587.00	15331.00	4500.00	40000.00
4-Year or Master's Level	142852.17	60623.00	0.00	822000.00
PHD & Research University	240046.73	109286.00	50000.00	1100000.00

3.8. Mean, Median, Minimum and Maximum Library Spending on Electronic Materials/Content in 2005 (in $), Broken Out by Public or Private Status of the College

Public or Private Status	Mean	Median	Minimum	Maximum
Public College	227014.67	40000.00	0.00	1100000.00
Private College	104814.92	53257.00	4500.00	465000.00

3.9. Mean, Median, Minimum and Maximum Number of Databases that the Library Tried on a Free Trial Basis Within the Past Year

	Mean	Median	Minimum	Maximum
All Libraries	5.68	4.00	0.00	20.00

3.10. Mean, Median, Minimum and Maximum Number of Databases that the Library Tried on a Free Trial Basis Within the Past Year, Broken Out by College Enrollment

Number of Enrolled Students (FTE)	Mean	Median	Minimum	Maximum
Less than 1,650	3.84	3.00	0.00	12.00
1650 -- 4,000	7.15	5.00	0.00	20.00
Greater than 4,000	7.63	5.50	0.00	20.00

3.11. Mean, Median, Minimum and Maximum Number of Databases that the Library Tried on a Free Trial Basis Within the Past Year, Broken Out by Type of College

Type of College	Mean	Median	Minimum	Maximum
Community College	5.43	3.00	2.00	18.00
4-Year or Master's Level	5.20	4.00	0.00	20.00
PHD & Research University	6.54	5.00	0.00	20.00

3.12. Mean, Median, Minimum and Maximum Number of Databases that the Library Tried on a Free Trial Basis Within the Past Year, Broken Out by Public or Private Status of the College

Public or Private Status	Mean	Median	Minimum	Maximum
Public College	5.64	5.00	0.00	18.00
Private College	5.69	4.00	0.00	20.00

3.13. Mean, Median, Minimum and Maximum Number of Databases Initially Tried on a Free Trial Basis Within the Past Year that the Library Subsequently Subscribed to

	Mean	Median	Minimum	Maximum
All Libraries	2.02	1.00	0.00	16.00

3.14. Mean, Median, Minimum and Maximum Number of Databases Initially Tried on a Free Trial Basis Within the Past Year that the Library Subsequently Subscribed to, Broken Out by College Enrollment

Number of Enrolled Students (FTE)	Mean	Median	Minimum	Maximum
Less than 1,650	1.44	1.00	0.00	3.00
1650 -- 4,000	2.69	2.00	0.00	16.00
Greater than 4,000	2.75	1.50	0.00	8.00

3.15. Mean, Median, Minimum and Maximum Number of Databases Initially Tried on a Free Trial Basis Within the Past Year that the Library Subsequently Subscribed to, Broken Out by Type of College

Type of College	Mean	Median	Minimum	Maximum
Community College	3.71	2.00	0.00	16.00
4-Year or Master's Level	1.53	1.00	0.00	5.00
PHD & Research University	2.15	2.00	0.00	8.00

3.16. Mean, Median, Minimum and Maximum Number of Databases Initially Tried on a Free Trial Basis Within the Past Year that the Library Subsequently Subscribed to, Broken Out by Public or Private Status of the College

Public or Private Status	Mean	Median	Minimum	Maximum
Public College	2.93	2.00	0.00	16.00
Private College	1.68	1.00	0.00	8.00

4. CHAPTER FOUR: DATABASE ACCESS INTERRUPTION ISSUES

The libraries in the sample spent a mean of about 159.3 hours per year of staff time addressing problems related to the interruption of database access, or about 4 solid weeks of full time work. What is striking about the data is very dramatic differences in amount of time spent addressing such issues. Some libraries spent as much as 600 man hours while other spent none at all. It strikes us that this is an area for library trade associations, consortiums and other organizations to get together and pool their experiences. Some libraries could learn quite a bit from others in this sphere and substantial time and personnel savings can be accrued by pursuing best practices. Predictably, research and PHD-level granting institutions spent the most time, about 251 hours per year on average, but otherwise college size and time spent addressing these problems was not strongly related.

4.1. Mean, Median, Minimum and Maximum Number of Staff Man Hours Per Year Spent Addressing Problems Relating to the Interruption of Access to Databases

	Mean	Median	Minimum	Maximum
All Libraries	159.29	90.00	0.00	600.00

4.2. Mean, Median, Minimum and Maximum Number of Staff Man Hours Per Year Spent Addressing Problems Relating to the Interruption of Access to Databases, Broken Out by College Enrollment

Number of Enrolled Students (FTE)	Mean	Median	Minimum	Maximum
Less than 1,650	175.06	100.00	10.00	600.00
1650 -- 4,000	132.27	40.00	0.00	500.00
Greater than 4,000	163.43	90.00	25.00	500.00

4.3. Mean, Median, Minimum and Maximum Number of Staff Man Hours Per Year Spent Addressing Problems Relating to the Interruption of Access to Databases, Broken Out by Type of College

Type of College	Mean	Median	Minimum	Maximum
Community College	109.86	52.00	5.00	500.00
4-Year or Master's Level	120.53	100.00	10.00	500.00
PHD & Research University	250.64	100.00	0.00	600.00

4.4. Mean, Median, Minimum and Maximum Number of Staff Man Hours Per Year Spent Addressing Problems Relating to the Interruption of Access to Databases, Broken Out by Public or Private Status of the College

Public or Private Status	Mean	Median	Minimum	Maximum
Public College	204.50	95.00	5.00	600.00
Private College	135.70	80.00	0.00	500.00

The largest libraries in terms of enrollment base served were much more likely to cite "Publisher Claims of Non-Payment" as a reason for database access interruption. Seventy percent (70%) of libraries serving institutions with an enrollment base exceeding 4,000. cited this as a problem. Overall, a third of libraries considered this an occasional problem and none said that they usually or always have problems in this respect. Most said that they "never had a problem" with publisher claims of non-payment (26.91%) or that they rarely had a problem (40.48%). Public colleges had more problems in this respect than private colleges. More than half of public colleges said that they occasionally have a problem with database access interruption due to publisher claims of non payment.

4.5. Rating of Database Publisher Claim of Non-Payment as a Reason for Database Access Interruption

	Never a Problem	Rarely a Problem	Occasionally Have a Problem	Usually Have a Problem	Always Have a Problem
All Libraries	26.19%	40.48%	33.33%	0.00%	0.00%

4.6. Rating of Database Publisher Claim of Non-Payment as a Reason for Database Access Interruption, Broken Out by College Enrollment

Number of Enrolled Students (FTE)	Never a Problem	Rarely a Problem	Occasionally Have a Problem	Usually Have a Problem	Always Have a Problem
Less than 1,650	36.84%	36.84%	26.32%	0.00%	0.00%
1650 -- 4,000	23.08%	61.54%	15.38%	0.00%	0.00%
Greater than 4,000	10.00%	20.00%	70.00%	0.00%	0.00%

4.7. Rating of Database Publisher Claim of Non-Payment as a Reason for Database Access Interruption, Broken Out by Type of College

Type of College	Never a Problem	Rarely a Problem	Occasionally Have a Problem	Usually Have a Problem	Always Have a Problem
Community College	28.57%	42.86%	28.57%	0.00%	0.00%
4-Year or Master's Level	23.81%	42.86%	33.33%	0.00%	0.00%
PHD & Research University	28.57%	35.71%	35.71%	0.00%	0.00%

4.8. Rating of Database Publisher Claim of Non-Payment as a Reason for Database Access Interruption, Broken Out by Public or Private Status of the College

Public or Private Status	Never a Problem	Rarely a Problem	Occasionally Have a Problem	Usually Have a Problem	Always Have a Problem
Public College	13.33%	33.33%	53.33%	0.00%	0.00%
Private College	33.33%	44.44%	22.22%	0.00%	0.00%

Database access interruption stemming from changes in URL's by database vendors was a significant problem for the larger libraries in the sample, but not as much a problem for the small and medium sized libraries. More than half of the libraries serving an enrollment base of more than 4,000 said that they occasionally have a problem with changes in URL's while an astonishing 40% said that they usually have such problems. All of those colleges that said that they usually have such problems were PHD granting or research universities.

4.9. Rating of Database Publisher Changes of Access URL as a Reason for Database Access Interruption

	Never a Problem	Rarely a Problem	Occasionally Have a Problem	Usually Have a Problem	Always Have a Problem
All Libraries	21.95%	34.15%	34.15%	9.76%	0.00%

4.10. Rating of Database Publisher Changes of Access URL as a Reason for Database Access Interruption, Broken Out by College Enrollment

Number of Enrolled Students (FTE)	Never a Problem	Rarely a Problem	Occasionally Have a Problem	Usually Have a Problem	Always Have a Problem
Less than 1,650	27.78%	44.44%	27.78%	0.00%	0.00%
1650 -- 4,000	23.08%	46.15%	30.77%	0.00%	0.00%
Greater than 4,000	10.00%	0.00%	50.00%	40.00%	0.00%

4.11. Rating of Database Publisher Changes of Access URL as a Reason for Database Access Interruption, Broken Out by Type of College

Type of College	Never a Problem	Rarely a Problem	Occasionally Have a Problem	Usually Have a Problem	Always Have a Problem
Community College	28.57%	57.14%	14.29%	0.00%	0.00%
4-Year or Master's Level	25.00%	35.00%	40.00%	0.00%	0.00%
PHD & Research University	14.29%	21.43%	35.71%	28.57%	0.00%

4.12. Rating of Database Publisher Changes of Access URL as a Reason for Database Access Interruption, Broken Out by Public or Private Status of the College

Public or Private Status	Never a Problem	Rarely a Problem	Occasionally Have a Problem	Usually Have a Problem	Always Have a Problem
Public College	6.67%	20.00%	53.33%	20.00%	0.00%
Private College	30.77%	42.31%	23.08%	3.85%	0.00%

Many colleges still have problems with failures of their own computer networks as a reason for interruptions in database access. Community colleges in particular cited this as a reason for database access interruption.

4.13. Rating of College Network Malfunctions as a Reason for Database Access Interruption

	Never a Problem	Rarely a Problem	Occasionally Have a Problem	Usually Have a Problem	Always Have a Problem
All Libraries	0.00%	38.10%	52.38%	9.52%	0.00%

4.14. Rating of College Network Malfunctions as a Reason for Database Access Interruption, Broken Out by College Enrollment

Number of Enrolled Students (FTE)	Never a Problem	Rarely a Problem	Occasionally Have a Problem	Usually Have a Problem	Always Have a Problem
Less than 1,650	0.00%	26.32%	68.42%	5.26%	0.00%
1650 -- 4,000	0.00%	38.46%	46.15%	15.38%	0.00%
Greater than 4,000	0.00%	60.00%	30.00%	10.00%	0.00%

4.15. Rating of College Network Malfunctions as a Reason for Database Access Interruption, Broken Out by Type of College

Type of College	Never a Problem	Rarely a Problem	Occasionally Have a Problem	Usually Have a Problem	Always Have a Problem
Community College	0.00%	14.29%	71.43%	14.29%	0.00%
4-Year or Master's Level	0.00%	42.86%	57.14%	0.00%	0.00%
PHD & Research University	0.00%	42.86%	35.71%	21.43%	0.00%

4.16. Rating of College Network Malfunctions as a Reason for Database Access Interruption, Broken Out by Public or Private Status of the College

Public or Private Status	Never a Problem	Rarely a Problem	Occasionally Have a Problem	Usually Have a Problem	Always Have a Problem
Public College	0.00%	40.00%	46.67%	13.33%	0.00%
Private College	0.00%	37.04%	55.56%	7.41%	0.00%

4.17. Rating of Database Publisher Network Malfunctions as a Reason for Database Access Interruption

	Never a Problem	Rarely a Problem	Occasionally Have a Problem	Usually Have a Problem	Always Have a Problem
All Libraries	2.38%	38.10%	54.76%	4.76%	0.00%

4.18. Rating of Database Publisher Network Malfunctions as a Reason for Database Access Interruption, Broken Out by College Enrollment

Number of Enrolled Students (FTE)	Never a Problem	Rarely a Problem	Occasionally Have a Problem	Usually Have a Problem	Always Have a Problem
Less than 1,650	0.00%	36.84%	63.16%	0.00%	0.00%
1650 -- 4,000	0.00%	46.15%	53.85%	0.00%	0.00%
Greater than 4,000	10.00%	30.00%	40.00%	20.00%	0.00%

4.19. Rating of Database Publisher Network Malfunctions as a Reason for Database Access Interruption, Broken Out by Type of College

Type of College	Never a Problem	Rarely a Problem	Occasionally Have a Problem	Usually Have a Problem	Always Have a Problem
Community College	0.00%	28.57%	71.43%	0.00%	0.00%
4-Year or Master's Level	4.76%	38.10%	57.14%	0.00%	0.00%
PHD & Research University	0.00%	42.86%	42.86%	14.29%	0.00%

4.20. Rating of Database Publisher Network Malfunctions as a Reason for Database Access Interruption, Broken Out by Public or Private Status of the College

Public or Private Status	Never a Problem	Rarely a Problem	Occasionally Have a Problem	Usually Have a Problem	Always Have a Problem
Public College	6.67%	26.67%	60.00%	6.67%	0.00%
Private College	0.00%	44.44%	51.85%	3.70%	0.00%

5. CHAPTER FIVE: GRANTS & ENDOWMENTS FOR THE LIBRARY

Approximately 17.31% of the libraries in the sample have received a grant from state or local government within the past year, and most recipients were colleges with more than 4,000 enrolled students. Nearly 40% of the libraries of such colleges had received a grant from state or local government in the past year. 11.54% of the libraries in the sample received a grant from a private foundation, while 3.85% received a grant from a private company. 15.4% received a grant from a special fund sponsored by their college, and the same percentage received a grant from alumni.

5.1. Percentage of Libraries that Received a Grant from State or Local Governments Within the Past Year

	Yes	No
All Libraries	17.31%	82.69%

5.2. Percentage of Libraries that Received a Grant from State or Local Governments Within the Past Year, Broken Out by College Enrollment

Number of Enrolled Students (FTE)	Yes	No
Less than 1,650	14.29%	85.71%
1650 -- 4,000	5.88%	94.12%
Greater than 4,000	38.46%	61.54%

5.3. Percentage of Libraries that Received a Grant from State or Local Governments Within the Past Year, Broken Out by Type of College

Type of College	Yes	No
Community College	22.22%	77.78%
4-Year or Master's Level	19.23%	80.77%
PHD & Research University	12.50%	87.50%

5.4. Percentage of Libraries that Received a Grant from State or Local Governments Within the Past Year, Broken Out by Public or Private Status of the College

Public or Private Status	Yes	No
Public College	25.00%	75.00%
Private College	12.90%	87.10%

5.5.   Percentage of Libraries that Received a Grant from a Private Foundation Within the Past Year

	Yes	No
All Libraries	11.54%	88.46%

5.6.   Percentage of Libraries that Received a Grant from a Private Foundation Within the Past Year, Broken Out by College Enrollment

Number of Enrolled Students (FTE)	Yes	No
Less than 1,650	9.52%	90.48%
1650 -- 4,000	11.76%	88.24%
Greater than 4,000	15.38%	84.62%

5.7.   Percentage of Libraries that Received a Grant from a Private Foundation Within the Past Year, Broken Out by Type of College

Type of College	Yes	No
Community College	0.00%	100.00%
4-Year or Master's Level	7.69%	92.31%
PHD & Research University	25.00%	75.00%

5.8.   Percentage of Libraries that Received a Grant from a Private Foundation Within the Past Year, Broken Out by Public or Private Status of the College

Public or Private Status	Yes	No
Public College	15.00%	85.00%
Private College	9.68%	90.32%

5.9.   Percentage of Libraries that Received a Grant from a Private Company Within the Past Year

	Yes	No
All Libraries	3.85%	96.15%

5.10.   Percentage of Libraries that Received a Grant from a Private Company Within the Past Year, Broken Out by College Enrollment

Number of Enrolled Students (FTE)	Yes	No
Less than 1,650	4.76%	95.24%
1650 -- 4,000	5.88%	94.12%
Greater than 4,000	0.00%	100.00%

5.11.   Percentage of Libraries that Received a Grant from a Private Company Within the Past Year, Broken Out by Type of College

Type of College	Yes	No
Community College	0.00%	100.00%
4-Year or Master's Level	7.69%	92.31%
PHD & Research University	0.00%	100.00%

5.12.   Percentage of Libraries that Received a Grant from a Private Company Within the Past Year, Broken Out by Public or Private Status of the College

Public or Private Status	Yes	No
Public College	0.00%	100.00%
Private College	6.45%	93.55%

5.13.   Percentage of Libraries that Received a Grant from a Special College Fund Within the Past Year

	Yes	No
All Libraries	15.38%	84.62%

5.14.   Percentage of Libraries that Received a Grant from a Special College Fund Within the Past Year, Broken Out by College Enrollment

Number of Enrolled Students (FTE)	Yes	No
Less than 1,650	14.29%	85.71%
1650 -- 4,000	5.88%	94.12%
Greater than 4,000	30.77%	69.23%

5.15.   Percentage of Libraries that Received a Grant from a Special College Fund Within the Past Year, Broken Out by Type of College

Type of College	Yes	No
Community College	0.00%	100.00%
4-Year or Master's Level	19.23%	80.77%
PHD & Research University	18.75%	81.25%

5.16.   Percentage of Libraries that Received a Grant from a Special College Fund Within the Past Year, Broken Out by Public or Private Status of the College

Public or Private Status	Yes	No
Public College	30.00%	70.00%
Private College	6.45%	93.55%

5.17. Percentage of Libraries that Received a Grant from Alumni Within the Past Year

	Yes	No
All Libraries	15.38%	84.62%

5.18. Percentage of Libraries that Received a Grant from Alumni Within the Past Year, Broken Out by College Enrollment

Number of Enrolled Students (FTE)	Yes	No
Less than 1,650	9.52%	90.48%
1650 -- 4,000	5.88%	94.12%
Greater than 4,000	38.46%	61.54%

5.19. Percentage of Libraries that Received a Grant from Alumni Within the Past Year, Broken Out by Type of College

Type of College	Yes	No
Community College	0.00%	100.00%
4-Year or Master's Level	19.23%	80.77%
PHD & Research University	18.75%	81.25%

5.20. Percentage of Libraries that Received a Grant from Alumni Within the Past Year, Broken Out by Public or Private Status of the College

Public or Private Status	Yes	No
Public College	25.00%	75.00%
Private College	9.68%	90.32%

5.21. Percentage of Libraries that Received a Grant from Any Other Source Not Previously Cited Within the Past Year

	Yes	No
All Libraries	5.77%	94.23%

5.22. Percentage of Libraries that Received a Grant from Any Other Source Not Previously Cited Within the Past Year, Broken Out by College Enrollment

Number of Enrolled Students (FTE)	Yes	No
Less than 1,650	9.52%	90.48%
1650 -- 4,000	0.00%	100.00%
Greater than 4,000	7.69%	92.31%

5.23.   Percentage of Libraries that Received a Grant from Any Other Source Not Previously Cited Within the Past Year, Broken Out by Type of College

Type of College	Yes	No
Community College	22.22%	77.78%
4-Year or Master's Level	0.00%	100.00%
PHD & Research University	6.25%	93.75%

5.24.   Percentage of Libraries that Received a Grant from Any Other Source Not Previously Cited Within the Past Year, Broken Out by Public or Private Status of the College

Public or Private Status	Yes	No
Public College	10.00%	90.00%
Private College	3.23%	96.77%

Grant income can be volatile: the mean value of spending derived from grants for the libraries in the sample was $12,332 in 2005 but more than $50,000 in 2006. Most libraries in the sample had no grant income but a substantial minority did. Community colleges had a mean of only about $2,200 in grant derived spending while the PHD granting and research –level research libraries in the sample garnered more than 10 times this sum.

The libraries in the sample spent a mean of 59.55 man hours in preparing grants, with a median of only 22.5 hours. The key variable in how much time a college spent appears to be college size rather than college type, and community colleges actually spent more time than others in grant applications, though they appear to be far less successful than other types of colleges in actually winning the grants. It may be that many grants are connected to more sophisticated or intricate library technologies or practices less likely to be used by community colleges, but the question perhaps merits further investigation. Are community colleges getting their fair share of library grant money? Perhaps not. They apply for fewer grants but spend more time doing so than their peers in other institutions. It may be that workshops aimed at grant writing skills may be needed on the community college level since grant writing is not a specialty that many community colleges can actually afford.

Most of the libraries in the sample receive at least some revenue from special endowments. As might be expected, the libraries serving a larger student enrolled base receive far more from endowments, by a factor of 5 or 6, than smaller academic libraries. Few community colleges enjoyed endowment income. Interestingly, the public colleges in the sample had higher mean income from endowments than the private colleges, though one very high outlier may have caused this. Median income from endowments was higher among the private college than the public college libraries.

More than a quarter of the libraries in the sample enjoyed special endowments targeted at building book collections while less than 10% had endowments targeted at electronic resources. Nonetheless, since these resources have a much shorter history, coming into use in substantial ways only in the 1990's, one might say that they have already started to catch up to books in the world of dedicated endowments.

More than 23% of libraries in the sample had endowments targeted at specific subjects while less than 16% had endowments for special collection, and most of these were PHD-granting or research level universities.

5.25. Mean, Median, Minimum and Maximum Total Value of Spending Derived from Grants, 2005 (in $)

	Mean	Median	Minimum	Maximum
All Libraries	12332.39	1250.00	0.00	100000.00

5.26. Mean, Median, Minimum and Maximum Total Value of Spending Derived from Grants (in $), Broken Out by College Enrollment, 2005

Number of Enrolled Students (FTE)	Mean	Median	Minimum	Maximum
Less than 1,650	3507.00	0.00	0.00	16150.00
1650 -- 4,000	13567.33	500.00	0.00	85508.00
Greater than 4,000	32650.43	15000.00	0.00	100000.00

5.27. Mean, Median, Minimum and Maximum Total Value of Spending Derived from Grants (in $), Broken Out by Type of College, 2005

Type of College	Mean	Median	Minimum	Maximum
Community College	2200.00	0.00	0.00	8300.00
4-Year or Master's Level	11162.71	5000.00	0.00	85508.00
PHD & Research University	21909.09	0.00	0.00	100000.00

5.28. Mean, Median, Minimum and Maximum Total Value of Spending Derived from Grants (in $), Broken Out by Public or Private Status of the College, 2005

Public or Private Status	Mean	Median	Minimum	Maximum
Public College	19129.42	1500.00	0.00	100000.00
Private College	9746.05	3127.50	0.00	85508.00

5.29. Mean, Median, Minimum and Maximum Total Value of Spending Derived from Grants (in $), 2006

	Mean	Median	Minimum	Maximum
All Libraries	50055.00	0.00	0.00	1042056.00

5.30. Mean, Median, Minimum and Maximum Total Value of Spending Derived from Grants 2006 (in $), Broken Out by College Enrollment

Number of Enrolled Students (FTE)	Mean	Median	Minimum	Maximum
Less than 1,650	2751.00	0.00	0.00	11133.00
1650 -- 4,000	97486.91	0.00	0.00	1042056.00
Greater than 4,000	90793.29	25000.00	0.00	411553.00

5.31. Mean, Median, Minimum and Maximum Total Value of Spending Derived from Grants 2006 (in $), Broken Out by Type of College

Type of College	Mean	Median	Minimum	Maximum
Community College	3880.86	0.00	0.00	11133.00
4-Year or Master's Level	95547.44	3425.00	0.00	1042056.00
PHD & Research University	17818.18	0.00	0.00	100000.00

5.32. Mean, Median, Minimum and Maximum Total Value of Spending Derived from Grants 2006 (in $), Broken Out by Public or Private Status of the College

Public or Private Status	Mean	Median	Minimum	Maximum
Public College	57777.55	2000.00	0.00	411553.00
Private College	48537.91	0.00	0.00	1042056.00

The libraries in the sample spent a mean of only 59.55 hours in staff time annually in preparing grants for the library; the median was only 22.5 hours.

5.33. Mean, Median, Minimum and Maximum Time in Man Hours Spent in Preparing Grants for the Library

	Mean	Median	Minimum	Maximum
All Libraries	59.55	22.50	0.00	500.00

5.34. Mean, Median, Minimum and Maximum Time in Man Hours Spent in Preparing Grants for the Library, Broken Out by College Enrollment

Number of Enrolled Students (FTE)	Mean	Median	Minimum	Maximum
Less than 1,650	50.44	10.00	0.00	200.00
1650 -- 4,000	45.42	17.50	0.00	200.00
Greater than 4,000	103.22	39.00	0.00	500.00

5.35. Mean, Median, Minimum and Maximum Time in Man Hours Spent in Preparing Grants for the Library, Broken Out by Type of College

Type of College	Mean	Median	Minimum	Maximum
Community College	65.43	8.00	0.00	200.00
4-Year or Master's Level	58.70	27.00	0.00	500.00
PHD & Research University	62.50	32.50	0.00	200.00

5.36. Mean, Median, Minimum and Maximum Time in Man Hours Spent in Preparing Grants for the Library, Broken Out by Public or Private Status of the College

Public or Private Status	Mean	Median	Minimum	Maximum
Public College	75.31	35.00	0.00	500.00
Private College	53.96	20.00	0.00	200.00

5.37. Mean, Median, Minimum and Maximum Number of Grants Applied for in the Past Year

	Mean	Median	Minimum	Maximum
All Libraries	1.50	1.00	0.00	15.00

5.38. Mean, Median, Minimum and Maximum Number of Grants Applied for in the Past Year, Broken Out by College Enrollment

Number of Enrolled Students (FTE)	Mean	Median	Minimum	Maximum
Less than 1,650	1.16	1.00	0.00	4.00
1650 -- 4,000	0.75	0.50	0.00	3.00
Greater than 4,000	3.63	1.50	0.00	15.00

5.39. Mean, Median, Minimum and Maximum Number of Grants Applied for in the Past Year, Broken Out by Type of College

Type of College	Mean	Median	Minimum	Maximum
Community College	0.86	1.00	0.00	3.00
4-Year or Master's Level	2.00	1.00	0.00	15.00
PHD & Research University	1.23	1.00	0.00	6.00

5.40. Mean, Median, Minimum and Maximum Number of Grants Applied for in the Past Year, Broken Out by Public or Private Status of the College

Public or Private Status	Mean	Median	Minimum	Maximum
Public College	2.31	1.00	0.00	15.00
Private College	1.15	1.00	0.00	4.00

The libraries in the sample accrued a mean of only $12,166 from special endowments in the past year, with a median of $2,500.

5.41. Mean, Median, Minimum and Maximum Funds Accrued from Special Endowments in the Past Year (in $)

	Mean	Median	Minimum	Maximum
All Libraries	12166.50	2500.00	0.00	123000.00

5.42. Mean, Median, Minimum and Maximum Funds Accrued from Special Endowments in the Past Year (in $), Broken Out by College Enrollment

Number of Enrolled Students (FTE)	Mean	Median	Minimum	Maximum
Less than 1,650	6523.80	1300.00	0.00	52000.00
1650 -- 4,000	7617.55	2050.00	0.00	52575.51
Greater than 4,000	32494.57	25000.00	10.00	123000.00

5.43. Mean, Median, Minimum and Maximum Funds Accrued from Special Endowments in the Past Year (in $), Broken Out by Type of College

Type of College	Mean	Median	Minimum	Maximum
Community College	100.00	0.00	0.00	500.00
4-Year or Master's Level	11883.91	3600.00	0.00	52575.51
PHD & Research University	19168.36	2500.00	0.00	123000.00

5.44. Mean, Median, Minimum and Maximum Funds Accrued from Special Endowments in the Past Year (in $), Broken Out by Public or Private Status of the College

Public or Private Status	Mean	Median	Minimum	Maximum
Public College	18473.64	2100.00	0.00	123000.00
Private College	9442.12	2857.00	0.00	52575.51

5.45. Percentage of Libraries with Special Endowments Targeted at Book Collections

	Yes	No
All Libraries	26.92%	73.08%

5.46. Percentage of Libraries with Special Endowments Targeted at Book Collections, Broken Out by College Enrollment

Number of Enrolled Students (FTE)	Yes	No
Less than 1,650	23.81%	76.19%
1650 -- 4,000	11.76%	88.24%
Greater than 4,000	53.85%	46.15%

5.47. Percentage of Libraries with Special Endowments Targeted at Book Collections, Broken Out by Type of College

Type of College	Yes	No
Community College	11.11%	88.89%
4-Year or Master's Level	30.77%	69.23%
PHD & Research University	31.25%	68.75%

5.48. Percentage of Libraries with Special Endowments Targeted at Book Collections, Broken Out by Public or Private Status of the College

Public or Private Status	Yes	No
Public College	30.00%	70.00%
Private College	25.81%	74.19%

5.49. Percentage of Libraries with Special Endowments Targeted at Electronic Resources

	Yes	No
All Libraries	9.62%	90.38%

5.50. Percentage of Libraries with Special Endowments Targeted at Electronic Resources, Broken Out by College Enrollment

Number of Enrolled Students (FTE)	Yes	No
Less than 1,650	9.52%	90.48%
1650 -- 4,000	0.00%	100.00%
Greater than 4,000	23.08%	76.92%

5.51. Percentage of Libraries with Special Endowments Targeted at Electronic Resources, Broken Out by Type of College

Type of College	Yes	No
Community College	0.00%	100.00%
4-Year or Master's Level	15.38%	84.62%
PHD & Research University	6.25%	93.75%

5.52. Percentage of Libraries with Special Endowments Targeted at Electronic Resources, Broken Out by Public or Private Status of the College

Public or Private Status	Yes	No
Public College	15.00%	85.00%
Private College	6.45%	93.55%

5.53. Percentage of Libraries with Special Endowments Targeted at Specific Academic Subject Fields

	Yes	No
All Libraries	23.08%	76.92%

5.54. Percentage of Libraries with Special Endowments Targeted at Specific Academic Subject Fields, Broken Out by College Enrollment

Number of Enrolled Students (FTE)	Yes	No
Less than 1,650	9.52%	90.48%
1650 -- 4,000	11.76%	88.24%
Greater than 4,000	61.54%	38.46%

5.55. Percentage of Libraries with Special Endowments Targeted at Specific Academic Subject Fields, Broken Out by Type of College

Type of College	Yes	No
Community College	0.00%	100.00%
4-Year or Master's Level	23.08%	76.92%
PHD & Research University	37.50%	62.50%

5.56. Percentage of Libraries with Special Endowments Targeted at Specific Academic Subject Fields, Broken Out by Public or Private Status of the College

Public or Private Status	Yes	No
Public College	35.00%	65.00%
Private College	16.13%	83.87%

5.57. Percentage of Libraries with Special Endowments Targeted at Special Collections

	Yes	No
All Libraries	15.38%	84.62%

5.58. Percentage of Libraries with Special Endowments Targeted at Special Collections, Broken Out by College Enrollment

Number of Enrolled Students (FTE)	Yes	No
Less than 1,650	9.52%	90.48%
1650 -- 4,000	11.76%	88.24%
Greater than 4,000	30.77%	69.23%

5.59.   Percentage of Libraries with Special Endowments Targeted at Special Collections, Broken Out by Type of College

Type of College	Yes	No
Community College	0.00%	100.00%
4-Year or Master's Level	7.69%	92.31%
PHD & Research University	37.50%	62.50%

5.60.   Percentage of Libraries with Special Endowments Targeted at Special Collections, Broken Out by Public or Private Status of the College

Public or Private Status	Yes	No
Public College	15.00%	85.00%
Private College	16.13%	83.87%

6. CHAPTER SIX: USE OF CONSORTIUMS

Subscriptions obtained through consortiums account for a mean of 67% and a median of 75% of the database subscriptions maintained by the libraries in the sample. Community colleges went directly to publishers more often than other types of colleges: consortium purchases accounted for a bit less than 58% of their database subscriptions. Private colleges went through consortiums for close to three quarters of their database subscriptions, while for public colleges the corresponding figure was 55%. What is perhaps so striking is the enormous spread between the many libraries that do not use consortiums virtually at all and those that use them almost exclusively.

Overall, the library's largest consortium partner accounted for approximately 61.4% of total database spending, while the second largest consortium partner accounted for 14.3% of library database spending. Other consortium partners accounted for 4.84% of total library database spending.

6.1. Mean, Median, Minimum and Maximum Percentage of Library Database Subscriptions Accounted for by Subscriptions Through Consortiums

	Mean	Median	Minimum	Maximum
All Libraries	67.61	77.50	0.00	100.00

6.2. Mean, Median, Minimum and Maximum Percentage of Library Database Subscriptions Accounted for by Subscriptions Through Consortiums, Broken Out by College Enrollment

Number of Enrolled Students (FTE)	Mean	Median	Minimum	Maximum
Less than 1,650	72.50	90.00	0.00	100.00
1650 -- 4,000	54.61	57.00	0.00	100.00
Greater than 4,000	73.88	85.00	0.00	95.00

6.3. Mean, Median, Minimum and Maximum Percentage of Library Database Subscriptions Accounted for by Subscriptions Through Consortiums, Broken Out by Type of College

Type of College	Mean	Median	Minimum	Maximum
Community College	57.86	80.00	0.00	100.00
4-Year or Master's Level	73.06	88.00	70	100.00
PHD & Research University	64.67	72.50	0.00	100.00

6.4. Mean, Median, Minimum and Maximum Percentage of Library Database Subscriptions Accounted for by Subscriptions Through Consortiums, Broken Out by Public or Private Status of the College

Public or Private Status	Mean	Median	Minimum	Maximum
Public College	55.00	80.00	0.00	95.00
Private College	73.43	75.00	0.70	100.00

6.5. Mean, Median, Minimum and Maximum Percentage of the Library's Database Spending Accounted for by Spending Through the Library's Largest Consortium Partner

	Mean	Median	Minimum	Maximum
All Libraries	61.36	62.00	0.00	100.00

6.6. Mean, Median, Minimum and Maximum Percentage of the Library's Database Spending Accounted for by Spending Through the Library's Largest Consortium Partner, Broken Out by College Enrollment

Number of Enrolled Students (FTE)	Mean	Median	Minimum	Maximum
Less than 1,650	70.69	75.00	15.00	100.00
1650 -- 4,000	53.64	55.00	0.00	88.00
Greater than 4,000	61.00	62.00	0.00	100.00

6.7. Mean, Median, Minimum and Maximum Percentage of the Library's Database Spending Accounted for by Spending Through the Library's Largest Consortium Partner, Broken Out by Type of College

Type of College	Mean	Median	Minimum	Maximum
Community College	51.00	40.00	0.00	100.00
4-Year or Master's Level	68.42	70.00	29.00	100.00
PHD & Research University	59.45	60.00	0.00	95.00

6.8. Mean, Median, Minimum and Maximum Percentage of the Library's Database Spending Accounted for by Spending Through the Library's Largest Consortium Partner, Broken Out by Public or Private Status of the College

Public or Private Status	Mean	Median	Minimum	Maximum
Public College	47.90	45.00	0.00	100.00
Private College	69.20	70.00	33.00	100.00

6.9. Mean, Median, Minimum and Maximum Percentage of the Library's Database Spending Accounted for by Spending Through the Library's Second Largest Consortium Partner

	Mean	Median	Minimum	Maximum
All Libraries	14.30	12.50	0.00	40.00

6.10. Mean, Median, Minimum and Maximum Percentage of the Library's Database Spending Accounted for by Spending Through the Library's Second Largest Consortium Partner, Broken Out by College Enrollment

Number of Enrolled Students (FTE)	Mean	Median	Minimum	Maximum
Less than 1,650	19.68	18.50	2.00	40.00
1650 -- 4,000	15.39	15.00	0.00	40.00
Greater than 4,000	8.13	2.00	0.00	26.00

6.11. Mean, Median, Minimum and Maximum Percentage of the Library's Database Spending Accounted for by Spending Through the Library's Second Largest Consortium Partner, Broken Out by Type of College

Type of College	Mean	Median	Minimum	Maximum
Community College	16.67	10.00	0.00	40.00
4-Year or Master's Level	14.73	15.00	0.00	40.00
PHD & Research University	14.40	12.50	0.00	40.00

6.12. Mean, Median, Minimum and Maximum Percentage of the Library's Database Spending Accounted for by Spending Through the Library's Second Largest Consortium Partner, Broken Out by Public or Private Status of the College

Public or Private Status	Mean	Median	Minimum	Maximum
Public College	11.30	6.00	0.00	40.00
Private College	16.90	15.00	0.00	40.00

6.13. Mean, Median, Minimum and Maximum Percentage of the Library's Database Spending Accounted for by Spending Through the Library's Other Consortium Partners

	Mean	Median	Minimum	Maximum
All Libraries	4.84	0.00	0.00	35.00

6.14. Mean, Median, Minimum and Maximum Percentage of the Library's Database Spending Accounted for by Spending Through the Library's Other Consortium Partners, Broken Out by College Enrollment

Number of Enrolled Students (FTE)	Mean	Median	Minimum	Maximum
Less than 1,650	7.59	5.28	0.00	20.00
1650 -- 4,000	1.33	0.00	0.00	5.00
Greater than 4,000	8.00	1.50	0.00	35.00

6.15. Mean, Median, Minimum and Maximum Percentage of the Library's Database Spending Accounted for by Spending Through the Library's Other Consortium Partners, Broken Out by Type of College

Type of College	Mean	Median	Minimum	Maximum
Community College	0.00	0.00	0.00	0.00
4-Year or Master's Level	9.28	5.00	0.00	35.00
PHD & Research University	2.57	0.00	0.00	10.00

6.16. Mean, Median, Minimum and Maximum Percentage of the Library's Database Spending Accounted for by Spending Through the Library's Other Consortium Partners, Broken Out by Public or Private Status of the College

Public or Private Status	Mean	Median	Minimum	Maximum
Public College	6.00	0.00	0.00	35.00
Private College	5.36	5.00	0.00	20.00

7. CHAPTER SEVEN: LIBRARY WORKSTATIONS

The mean number of workstations maintained by the libraries in the sample primarily for use by librarians in 2005 was 22.8, increasing just slightly to 23 in 2006. In 2005 the libraries in the sample maintained a mean of 37.8 workstations for use by library patrons, a figure that rose to 41.8 in 2006 and will rise to 45.8 in 2007. Libraries have been adding patron workstations even as more libraries provide wireless access for students to use their own (or library-provided) laptop computers in the library. This tends to suggest that the expected reduction in the number of library workstations, caused by student use of their own laptops, may not happen, at least not in the near future. Indeed, the trend appears to be in the opposite direction, with increases in library workstations despite increased in-library wired laptop access.

The mean percentage of library workstations equipped with word processing software was about 61.1%. Libraries serving larger student populations were only somewhat more likely to offer word processing software on their workstations, though more than 69% of the library workstations offered by colleges that grant PHD's had word processing software. More than 82% of academic library workstations in the sample offered internet access though, for a handful of colleges fewer than 20% of their workstations offered internet access. Median levels of workstation internet access were 100% for most types of colleges. In general most colleges seem to have adopted the attitude that all workstations should offer broader internet access but a small minority of colleges still restrict most workstations to in-library resources.

A little less than half of the library workstations in the sample were equipped with presentation software and more than 82% offered access to at least some of the library's databases.

A shade more than 7% of the libraries in the sample had Compaq workstations, while more than 19.5% had workstations from Hewlett Packard, and more than three quarters had workstations from Dell, including 90% of those libraries serving an enrolled student base of greater than 4,000. Nearly 28% had workstations from IBM, including more than 42% of colleges in the sample serving an enrollment base of less than 1,650.

The library staff itself controls or is responsible for only about 46.8% of the total number of workstations in the library. The information technology department or its equivalent controls or is responsible for 81.2 % of library workstations. Overlapping responsibility appears to account for the data discrepancies, since the total of the percentage of workstations controlled by the library and the percentage controlled by the IT department exceeds 100%.

7.1. Mean, Median, Minimum and Maximum Number of Workstations Maintained by the Library Primarily for Use of Librarians, 2005

	Mean	Median	Minimum	Maximum
All Libraries	22.81	10.00	1.00	96.00

7.2. Mean, Median, Minimum and Maximum Number of Workstations Maintained by the Library Primarily for Use of Librarians, 2005, Broken Out by College Enrollment

Number of Enrolled Students (FTE)	Mean	Median	Minimum	Maximum
Less than 1,650	7.21	6.00	1.00	25.00
Private College	17.00	11.50	6.00	40.00
PHD & Research University	60.60	67.50	2.00	96.00

7.3. Mean, Median, Minimum and Maximum Number of Workstations Maintained by the Library Primarily for Use of Librarians, 2005, Broken Out by Type of College

Type of College	Mean	Median	Minimum	Maximum
Community College	4.14	3.00	1.00	11.00
4-Year or Master's Level	28.59	15.00	2.00	96.00
PHD & Research University	23.07	10.50	2.00	70.00

7.4. Mean, Median, Minimum and Maximum Number of Workstations Maintained by the Library Primarily for Use of Librarians, 2005, Broken Out by Public or Private Status of the College

Public or Private Status	Mean	Median	Minimum	Maximum
Public College	38.40	12.00	2.00	96.00
Private College	14.46	8.50	1.00	70.00

7.5. Mean, Median, Minimum and Maximum Number of Workstations Maintained by the Library Primarily for Use of Librarians, 2006

	Mean	Median	Minimum	Maximum
All Libraries	23.00	10.00	2.00	96.00

7.6. Mean, Median, Minimum and Maximum Number of Workstations Maintained by the Library Primarily for Use of Librarians, 2006, Broken Out by College Enrollment

Number of Enrolled Students (FTE)	Mean	Median	Minimum	Maximum
Less than 1,650	7.32	6.00	2.00	25.00
1650 -- 4,000	17.07	11.50	6.00	40.00
Greater than 4,000	61.10	70.00	2.00	96.00

7.7. Mean, Median, Minimum and Maximum Number of Workstations Maintained by the Library Primarily for Use of Librarians, 2006, Broken Out by Type of College

Type of College	Mean	Median	Minimum	Maximum
Community College	4.43	3.00	2.00	11.00
4-Year or Master's Level	28.59	15.00	2.00	96.00
PHD & Research University	23.50	10.50	2.00	70.00

7.8. Mean, Median, Minimum and Maximum Number of Workstations Maintained by the Library Primarily for Use of Librarians, 2006, Broken Out by Public or Private Status of the College

Public or Private Status	Mean	Median	Minimum	Maximum
Public College	38.73	12.00	2.00	96.00
Private College	14.57	8.50	2.00	70.00

7.9. Mean, Median, Minimum and Maximum Number of Workstations Maintained by the Library Primarily for Use of Library Patrons, 2005

	Mean	Median	Minimum	Maximum
All Libraries	37.78	24.00	1.00	130.00

7.10. Mean, Median, Minimum and Maximum Number of Workstations Maintained by the Library Primarily for Use of Library Patrons, 2005, Broken Out by College Enrollment

Number of Enrolled Students (FTE)	Mean	Median	Minimum	Maximum
Less than 1,650	21.50	15.00	2.00	120.00
Private College	47.50	39.50	15.00	130.00
PHD & Research University	55.22	54.00	1.00	110.00

7.11. Mean, Median, Minimum and Maximum Number of Workstations Maintained by the Library Primarily for Use of Library Patrons, 2005, Broken Out by Type of College

Type of College	Mean	Median	Minimum	Maximum
Community College	21.14	16.00	2.00	60.00
4-Year or Master's Level	45.62	33.00	8.00	130.00
PHD & Research University	34.08	24.00	1.00	110.00

7.12. Mean, Median, Minimum and Maximum Number of Workstations Maintained by the Library Primarily for Use of Library Patrons, 2005, Broken Out by Public or Private Status of the College

Public or Private Status	Mean	Median	Minimum	Maximum
Public College	45.15	50.00	1.00	92.00
Private College	34.36	19.50	2.00	130.00

7.13. Mean, Median, Minimum and Maximum Number of Workstations Maintained by the Library Primarily for Use of Library Patrons, 2006

	Mean	Median	Minimum	Maximum
All Libraries	41.77	27.00	1.00	135.00

7.14. Mean, Median, Minimum and Maximum Number of Workstations Maintained by the Library Primarily for Use of Library Patrons, 2006, Broken Out by College Enrollment

Number of Enrolled Students (FTE)	Mean	Median	Minimum	Maximum
Less than 1,650	21.37	16.00	1.00	120.00
1650 -- 4,000	52.07	47.50	15.00	130.00
Greater than 4,000	66.10	61.50	1.00	135.00

7.15. Mean, Median, Minimum and Maximum Number of Workstations Maintained by the Library Primarily for Use of Library Patrons, 2006, Broken Out by Type of College

Type of College	Mean	Median	Minimum	Maximum
Community College	22.71	18.00	2.00	65.00
4-Year or Master's Level	51.18	34.50	8.00	135.00
PHD & Research University	36.50	26.50	1.00	120.00

7.16. Mean, Median, Minimum and Maximum Number of Workstations Maintained by the Library Primarily for Use of Library Patrons, 2006, Broken Out by Public or Private Status of the College

Public or Private Status	Mean	Median	Minimum	Maximum
Public College	51.00	53.00	1.00	135.00
Private College	36.82	22.50	2.00	130.00

7.17. Mean, Median, Minimum and Maximum Number of Workstations Maintained by the Library Primarily for Use of Library Patrons, 2007

	Mean	Median	Minimum	Maximum
All Libraries	45.78	34.00	1.00	135.00

7.18. Mean, Median, Minimum and Maximum Number of Workstations Maintained by the Library Primarily for Use of Library Patrons, 2007, Broken Out by College Enrollment

Number of Enrolled Students (FTE)	Mean	Median	Minimum	Maximum
Less than 1,650	24.00	19.50	2.00	120.00
1650 -- 4,000	56.14	47.50	18.00	130.00
Greater than 4,000	73.22	78.00	1.00	135.00

7.19. Mean, Median, Minimum and Maximum Number of Workstations Maintained by the Library Primarily for Use of Library Patrons, 2007, Broken Out by Type of College

Type of College	Mean	Median	Minimum	Maximum
Community College	23.86	19.00	2.00	65.00
4-Year or Master's Level	52.00	34.50	8.00	135.00
PHD & Research University	47.17	42.50	1.00	125.00

7.20. Mean, Median, Minimum and Maximum Number of Workstations Maintained by the Library Primarily for Use of Library Patrons, 2007, Broken Out by Public or Private Status of the College

Public or Private Status	Mean	Median	Minimum	Maximum
Public College	58.69	65.00	1.00	135.00
Private College	39.79	28.50	2.00	130.00

7.21. Mean, Median, Minimum and Maximum Percentage of Library Workstations that Offer Internet Access

	Mean	Median	Minimum	Maximum
All Libraries	82.27	100.00	8.00	100.00

7.22. Mean, Median, Minimum and Maximum Percentage of Library Workstations that Offer Internet Access, Broken Out by College Enrollment

Number of Enrolled Students (FTE)	Mean	Median	Minimum	Maximum
Less than 1,650	79.83	100.00	8.00	100.00
1650 -- 4,000	75.73	100.00	16.00	100.00
Greater than 4,000	100.00	100.00	100.00	100.00

7.23. Mean, Median, Minimum and Maximum Percentage of Library Workstations that Offer Internet Access, Broken Out by Type of College

Type of College	Mean	Median	Minimum	Maximum
Community College	68.14	88.00	14.00	100.00
4-Year or Master's Level	80.91	100.00	8.00	100.00
PHD & Research University	93.00	100.00	16.00	100.00

7.24. Mean, Median, Minimum and Maximum Percentage of Library Workstations that Offer Internet Access, Broken Out by Public or Private Status of the College

Public or Private Status	Mean	Median	Minimum	Maximum
Public College	96.69	100.00	57.00	100.00
Private College	75.57	100.00	8.00	100.00

7.25. Mean, Median, Minimum and Maximum Percentage of Library Workstations that are Equipped with Word Processing Software

	Mean	Median	Minimum	Maximum
All Libraries	61.12	75.00	0.00	100.00

7.26. Mean, Median, Minimum and Maximum Percentage of Library Workstations that are Equipped with Word Processing Software, Broken Out by College Enrollment

Number of Enrolled Students (FTE)	Mean	Median	Minimum	Maximum
Less than 1,650	60.39	82.50	0.00	100.00
1650 -- 4,000	57.53	59.00	0.00	100.00
Greater than 4,000	69.50	98.00	0.00	100.00

7.27. Mean, Median, Minimum and Maximum Percentage of Library Workstations that are Equipped with Word Processing Software, Broken Out by Type of College

Type of College	Mean	Median	Minimum	Maximum
Community College	55.86	59.00	0.00	100.00
4-Year or Master's Level	60.86	72.50	0.00	100.00
PHD & Research University	64.67	100.00	0.00	100.00

7.28. Mean, Median, Minimum and Maximum Percentage of Library Workstations that are Equipped with Word Processing Software, Broken Out by Public or Private Status of the College

Public or Private Status	Mean	Median	Minimum	Maximum
Public College	78.08	100.00	0.00	100.00
Private College	53.25	49.50	0.00	100.00

7.29. Mean, Median, Minimum and Maximum Percentage of Library Workstations that are Equipped with Presentation Software

	Mean	Median	Minimum	Maximum
All Libraries	48.63	48.00	0.00	100.00

7.30. Mean, Median, Minimum and Maximum Percentage of Library Workstations that are Equipped with Presentation Software, Broken Out by College Enrollment

Number of Enrolled Students (FTE)	Mean	Median	Minimum	Maximum
Less than 1,650	49.83	40.00	0.00	100.00
1650 -- 4,000	49.13	48.00	0.00	100.00
Greater than 4,000	45.00	30.00	0.00	100.00

7.31. Mean, Median, Minimum and Maximum Percentage of Library Workstations that are Equipped with Presentation Software, Broken Out by Type of College

Type of College	Mean	Median	Minimum	Maximum
Community College	55.86	59.00	0.00	100.00
4-Year or Master's Level	37.59	24.00	0.00	100.00
PHD & Research University	64.67	100.00	0.00	100.00

7.32. Mean, Median, Minimum and Maximum Percentage of Library Workstations that are Equipped with Presentation Software, Broken Out by Public or Private Status of the College

Public or Private Status	Mean	Median	Minimum	Maximum
Public College	59.00	60.00	0.00	100.00
Private College	43.82	24.00	0.00	100.00

7.33. Mean, Median, Minimum and Maximum Percentage of Library Workstations that are Equipped with Access to Databases of Copyright Information and Content

	Mean	Median	Minimum	Maximum
All Libraries	82.27	100.00	8.00	100.00

7.34. Mean, Median, Minimum and Maximum Percentage of Library Workstations that are Equipped with Access to Databases of Copyright Information and Content, Broken Out by College Enrollment

Number of Enrolled Students (FTE)	Mean	Median	Minimum	Maximum
Less than 1,650	80.50	100.00	8.00	100.00
1650 -- 4,000	78.20	100.00	0.00	100.00
Greater than 4,000	100.00	100.00	100.00	100.00

7.35. Mean, Median, Minimum and Maximum Percentage of Library Workstations that are Equipped with Access to Databases of Copyright Information and Content, Broken Out by Type of College

Type of College	Mean	Median	Minimum	Maximum
Community College	69.86	100.00	14.00	100.00
4-Year or Master's Level	79.50	100.00	0.00	100.00
PHD & Research University	98.67	100.00	84.00	100.00

7.36. Mean, Median, Minimum and Maximum Percentage of Library Workstations that are Equipped with Access to Databases of Copyright Information and Content, Broken Out by Public or Private Status of the College

Public or Private Status	Mean	Median	Minimum	Maximum
Public College	96.69	100.00	57.00	100.00
Private College	77.32	100.00	0.00	100.00

7.37. Percentage of Libraries that have Workstations from Compaq

	Yes	No
All Libraries	7.14%	92.86%

7.38. Percentage of Libraries that have Workstations from Compaq, Broken Out by College Enrollment

Number of Enrolled Students (FTE)	Yes	No
Less than 1,650	11.11%	88.89%
1650 -- 4,000	0.00%	100.00%
Greater than 4,000	11.11%	88.89%

7.39. Percentage of Libraries that have Workstations from Compaq, Broken Out by Type of College

Type of College	Yes	No
Community College	14.29%	85.71%
4-Year or Master's Level	4.55%	95.45%
PHD & Research University	7.69%	92.31%

7.40. Percentage of Libraries that have Workstations from Compaq, Broken Out by Public or Private Status of the College

Public or Private Status	Yes	No
Public College	14.29%	85.71%
Private College	3.57%	96.43%

7.41. Percentage of Libraries that have Workstations from Hewlett Packard

	Yes	No
All Libraries	19.51%	80.49%

7.42. Percentage of Libraries that have Workstations from Hewlett Packard, Broken Out by College Enrollment

Number of Enrolled Students (FTE)	Yes	No
Less than 1,650	33.33%	66.67%
1650 -- 4,000	14.29%	85.71%
Greater than 4,000	0.00%	100.00%

7.43. Percentage of Libraries that have Workstations from Hewlett Packard, Broken Out by Type of College

Type of College	Yes	No
Community College	14.29%	85.71%
4-Year or Master's Level	23.81%	76.19%
PHD & Research University	15.38%	84.62%

7.44. Percentage of Libraries that have Workstations from Hewlett Packard, Broken Out by Public or Private Status of the College

Public or Private Status	Yes	No
Public College	0.00%	100.00%
Private College	28.57%	71.43%

7.45. Percentage of Libraries that have Workstations from Dell

	Yes	No
All Libraries	76.74%	23.26%

7.46. Percentage of Libraries that have Workstations from Dell, Broken Out by College Enrollment

Number of Enrolled Students (FTE)	Yes	No
Less than 1,650	66.67%	33.33%
1650 – 4,000	80.00%	20.00%
Greater than 4,000	90.00%	10.00%

7.47. Percentage of Libraries that have Workstations from Dell, Broken Out by Type of College

Type of College	Yes	No
Community College	42.86%	57.14%
4-Year or Master's Level	82.61%	17.39%
PHD & Research University	84.62%	15.38%

7.48. Percentage of Libraries that have Workstations from Dell, Broken Out by Public or Private Status of the College

Public or Private Status	Yes	No
Public College	81.25%	18.75%
Private College	74.07%	25.93%

7.49. Percentage of Libraries that have Workstations from IBM

	Yes	No
All Libraries	27.91%	72.09%

7.50. Percentage of Libraries that have Workstations from IBM, Broken Out by College Enrollment

Number of Enrolled Students (FTE)	Yes	No
Less than 1,650	42.11%	57.89%
1650 – 4,000	26.67%	73.33%
Greater than 4,000	0.00%	100.00%

7.51. Percentage of Libraries that have Workstations from IBM, Broken Out by Type of College

Type of College	Yes	No
Community College	42.86%	57.14%
4-Year or Master's Level	27.27%	72.73%
PHD & Research University	21.43%	78.57%

7.52. Percentage of Libraries that have Workstations from IBM, Broken Out by Public or Private Status of the College

Public or Private Status	Yes	No
Public College	6.67%	93.33%
Private College	39.29%	60.71%

7.53. Percentage of Libraries that have Workstations from Other Manufacturers not Previously Cited

	Yes	No
All Libraries	27.27%	72.73%

7.54. Percentage of Libraries that have Workstations from Other Manufacturers not Previously Cited, Broken Out by College Enrollment

Number of Enrolled Students (FTE)	Yes	No
Less than 1,650	26.32%	73.68%
1650 -- 4,000	40.00%	60.00%
Greater than 4,000	10.00%	90.00%

7.55. Percentage of Libraries that have Workstations from Other Manufacturers not Previously Cited, Broken Out by Type of College

Type of College	Yes	No
Community College	28.57%	71.43%
4-Year or Master's Level	30.43%	69.57%
PHD & Research University	21.43%	78.57%

7.56. Percentage of Libraries that have Workstations from Other Manufacturers not Previously Cited, Broken Out by Public or Private Status of the College

Public or Private Status	Yes	No
Public College	12.50%	87.50%
Private College	35.71%	64.29%

7.57. Mean, Median, Minimum and Maximum Percentage of Library Workstations Actually Controlled by the Library

	Mean	Median	Minimum	Maximum
All Libraries	46.83	25.00	0.00	100.00

7.58. Mean, Median, Minimum and Maximum Percentage of Library Workstations Actually Controlled by the Library, Broken Out by College Enrollment

Number of Enrolled Students (FTE)	Mean	Median	Minimum	Maximum
Less than 1,650	40.08	20.00	0.00	100.00
1650 -- 4,000	47.43	25.00	0.00	100.00
Greater than 4,000	63.13	75.00	5.00	100.00

7.59. Mean, Median, Minimum and Maximum Percentage of Library Workstations Actually Controlled by the Library, Broken Out by Type of College

Type of College	Mean	Median	Minimum	Maximum
Community College	32.50	15.00	0.00	100.00
4-Year or Master's Level	61.64	89.00	0.00	100.00
PHD & Research University	36.50	25.00	0.00	100.00

7.60. Mean, Median, Minimum and Maximum Percentage of Library Workstations Actually Controlled by the Library, Broken Out by Public or Private Status of the College

Public or Private Status	Mean	Median	Minimum	Maximum
Public College	51.92	40.00	0.00	100.00
Private College	45.53	25.00	0.00	100.00

7.61. Mean, Median, Minimum and Maximum Percentage of Library Workstations Actually Controlled by the College IT Department

	Mean	Median	Minimum	Maximum
All Libraries	81.17	100.00	0.00	100.00

7.62. Mean, Median, Minimum and Maximum Percentage of Library Workstations Actually Controlled by the College IT Department, Broken Out by College Enrollment

Number of Enrolled Students (FTE)	Mean	Median	Minimum	Maximum
Less than 1,650	78.69	96.00	0.00	100.00
1650 -- 4,000	89.85	100.00	22.00	100.00
Greater than 4,000	70.71	75.00	0.00	100.00

7.63. Mean, Median, Minimum and Maximum Percentage of Library Workstations Actually Controlled by the College IT Department, Broken Out by Type of College

Type of College	Mean	Median	Minimum	Maximum
Community College	95.00	100.00	80.00	100.00
4-Year or Master's Level	74.28	96.00	0.00	100.00
PHD & Research University	84.58	97.50	40.00	100.00

7.64. Mean, Median, Minimum and Maximum Percentage of Library Workstations Actually Controlled by the College IT Department, Broken Out by Public or Private Status of the College

Public or Private Status	Mean	Median	Minimum	Maximum
Public College	75.42	85.00	0.00	100.00
Private College	84.04	100.00	0.00	100.00

8. CHAPTER EIGHT: PERIODICALS SUBSCRIPTION AGENTS

About 79% of periodicals spending by the libraries in the sample is accounted for by spending through subscription agents. Approximately 85% of this spending is accounted for by spending through the single largest subscription agent maintained by the library. However, this figure includes libraries that do not use subscription agents so in many cases the median figure is a better guide. The median percentage of periodicals spending through subscription agents spent on the library's single largest agent was 97.5%. Most libraries pay their subscription agents in a lump sum at the beginning of the year, but a small minority, a bit less than 13%, pay their agents in increments throughout the year.

8.1. Mean, Median, Minimum and Maximum Percentage of Periodicals Spending Accounted for by Spending Through Consortiums

	Mean	Median	Minimum	Maximum
All Libraries	78.91	90.00	0.00	100.00

8.2. Mean, Median, Minimum and Maximum Percentage of Periodicals Spending Accounted for by Spending Through Subscription Agents, Broken Out by College Enrollment

Number of Enrolled Students (FTE)	Mean	Median	Minimum	Maximum
Less than 1,650	75.01	90.00	0.00	100.00
1650 -- 4,000	85.95	90.00	43.30	100.00
Greater than 4,000	57.75	80.00	0.00	100.00

8.3. Mean, Median, Minimum and Maximum Percentage of Periodicals Spending Accounted for by Spending Through Subscription Agents, Broken Out by Type of College

Type of College	Mean	Median	Minimum	Maximum
Community College	58.86	90.00	0.00	99.00
4-Year or Master's Level	87.79	95.00	43.30	100.00
PHD & Research University	75.38	85.00	0.00	98.00

8.4. Mean, Median, Minimum and Maximum Percentage of Periodicals Spending Accounted for by Spending Through Subscription Agents, Broken Out by Public or Private Status of the College

Public or Private Status	Mean	Median	Minimum	Maximum
Public College	76.54	90.00	0.00	100.00
Private College	80.02	90.00	0.00	100.00

8.5. Mean, Median, Minimum and Maximum Percentage of Periodicals Spending Through Subscription Agents Accounted for by Spending Through the Single Largest Subscription Agent

	Mean	Median	Minimum	Maximum
All Libraries	84.72	97.50	0.00	100.00

8.6. Mean, Median, Minimum and Maximum Percentage of Periodicals Spending Through Subscription Agents Accounted for by Spending Through the Single Largest Subscription Agent, Broken Out by College Enrollment

Number of Enrolled Students (FTE)	Mean	Median	Minimum	Maximum
Less than 1,650	73.60	90.00	0.00	100.00
1650 -- 4,000	97.57	99.00	90.00	100.00
Greater than 4,000	87.25	97.50	45.00	100.00

8.7. Mean, Median, Minimum and Maximum Percentage of Periodicals Spending Through Subscription Agents Accounted for by Spending Through the Single Largest Subscription Agent, Broken Out by Type of College

Type of College	Mean	Median	Minimum	Maximum
Community College	54.00	60.00	0.00	100.00
4-Year or Master's Level	91.13	100.00	50.00	100.00
PHD & Research University	91.45	98.00	45.00	100.00

8.8. Mean, Median, Minimum and Maximum Percentage of Periodicals Spending Through Subscription Agents Accounted for by Spending Through the Single Largest Subscription Agent, Broken Out by Public or Private Status of the College

Public or Private Status	Mean	Median	Minimum	Maximum
Public College	81.75	94.00	30.00	100.00
Private College	85.99	97.50	0.00	100.00

8.9. Timing of Payments to Subscription Agents

	Lump Sum at the Beginning of the Year	Payment in Increments
All Libraries	87.18%	12.82%

8.10. Timing of Payments to Subscription Agents, Broken Out by College Enrollment

Number of Enrolled Students (FTE)	Lump Sum at the Beginning of the Year	Payment in Increments
Less than 1,650	81.25%	18.75%
1650 -- 4,000	92.86%	7.14%
Greater than 4,000	88.89%	11.11%

8.11. Timing of Payments to Subscription Agents, Broken Out by Type of College

Type of College	Lump Sum at the Beginning of the Year	Payment in Increments
Community College	80.00%	20.00%
4-Year or Master's Level	86.36%	13.64%
PHD & Research University	91.67%	8.33%

8.12. Timing of Payments to Subscription Agents, Broken Out by Public or Private Status of the College

Public or Private Status	Lump Sum at the Beginning of the Year	Payment in Increments
Public College	84.62%	15.38%
Private College	88.46%	11.54%

9. CHAPTER NINE: LIBRARY TECHNOLOGY CENTERS

More than 40% of the libraries in the sample have a center or specific set of workstations earmarked for computer or information literacy of some kind. The larger the enrollment base served by the library, the more likely that library will have such a center of set of earmarked workstations specifically designed for information or computer literacy applications.   Surprisingly, none of the community colleges in the sample had such a center, a glaring lack since community college students often lag those in other colleges in levels of computer and information literacy.   Private colleges were more likely than public colleges to have such centers. The far underside of the digital divide includes more public college students than private college students so it seems that this may be an area that public colleges need to address.

The mean number of workstations in the technology center was a respectable 30.94 with a median of 26.5. Colleges serving an enrollment base of less than 1,650 actually had considerably more workstations in their technology center than those serving between 1,650 and 4,000 students. We suspect that this is because many colleges in the "fewer than 1,650" category are small, private liberal arts colleges that take information and computer literacy more seriously than others, or at least dedicate the resources to it.

9.1. Percentage of Libraries that Offer a Center or Set of Workstations Specifically Designed to Teach Students Information Technology

	Yes	No
All Libraries	40.00%	60.00%

9.2. Percentage of Libraries that Offer a Center or Set of Workstations Specifically Designed to Teach Students Information Technology, Broken Out by College Enrollment

Number of Enrolled Students (FTE)	Yes	No
Less than 1,650	22.22%	77.78%
1650 -- 4,000	50.00%	50.00%
Greater than 4,000	66.67%	33.33%

9.3. Percentage of Libraries that Offer a Center or Set of Workstations Specifically Designed to Teach Students Information Technology, Broken Out by Type of College

Type of College	Yes	No
Community College	0.00%	100.00%
4-Year or Master's Level	45.45%	54.55%
PHD & Research University	58.33%	41.67%

9.4. Percentage of Libraries that Offer a Center or Set of Workstations Specifically Designed to Teach Students Information Technology, Broken Out by Public or Private Status of the College

Public or Private Status	Yes	No
Public College	38.46%	61.54%
Private College	42.86%	57.14%

9.5. Mean, Median, Minimum and Maximum Number of Workstations in the Library Information Technology Center

	Mean	Median	Minimum	Maximum
All Libraries	30.94	26.50	7.00	80.00

9.6. Mean, Median, Minimum and Maximum Number of Workstations in the Library Information Technology Center, Broken Out by College Enrollment

Number of Enrolled Students (FTE)	Mean	Median	Minimum	Maximum
Less than 1,650	34.00	25.00	11.00	80.00
1650 -- 4,000	18.29	12.00	7.00	40.00
Greater than 4,000	43.17	35.00	15.00	80.00

9.7. Mean, Median, Minimum and Maximum Number of Workstations in the Library Information Technology Center, Broken Out by Type of College

Type of College	Mean	Median	Minimum	Maximum
Community College	14.00	14.00	14.00	14.00
4-Year or Master's Level	28.50	23.00	7.00	80.00
PHD & Research University	36.86	30.00	9.00	80.00

9.8. Mean, Median, Minimum and Maximum Number of Workstations in the Library Information Technology Center, Broken Out by Public or Private Status of the College

Public or Private Status	Mean	Median	Minimum	Maximum
Public College	35.80	30.00	15.00	66.00
Private College	29.08	21.00	7.00	80.00

10. CHAPTER TEN: BOOKS, Print & E-Books

The libraries in the sample spent a mean of $76,045 on books in 2005, and increased this spending slightly to $81,079 in 2006, an increase of 6.6%. Anticipated mean spending for 2007 was $80,090, a decline of about 1.2%.

While spending on traditional books has grown slowly, spending on e-books has continued to maintain relatively high growth rates, though total e-book spending is still a fraction of spending on traditional print books. E-book spending by the libraries in the sample increased from $6,692 in 2005 to $7,370 in 2006, and to an anticipated $8,706 in 2007, a two year increase of 30%. Also, e-book spending by the libraries in the sample has increased to approximately 11% of the level of traditional books spending, a figure that could easily grow to 20% of traditional book spending within five years, if recent patterns persist.

10.1. Mean, Median, Minimum and Maximum Library Spending on Books, 2005 (in $)

	Mean	Median	Minimum	Maximum
All Libraries	76045.21	59000.00	0.00	350000.00

10.2. Mean, Median, Minimum and Maximum Library Spending on Books 2005 (in $), Broken Out by College Enrollment

Number of Enrolled Students (FTE)	Mean	Median	Minimum	Maximum
Less than 1,650	39261.80	31454.00	0.00	92139.00
1650 -- 4,000	103852.00	85000.00	29500.00	192420.00
Greater than 4,000	106305.38	68208.00	5.00	350000.00

10.3. Mean, Median, Minimum and Maximum Library Spending on Books 2005 (in $), Broken Out by Type of College

Type of College	Mean	Median	Minimum	Maximum
Community College	20242.33	18500.00	0.00	42000.00
4-Year or Master's Level	70991.44	54250.00	5.00	190548.00
PHD & Research University	118244.20	77500.00	3000.00	350000.00

10.4. Mean, Median, Minimum and Maximum Library Spending on Books 2005 (in $), Broken Out by Public or Private Status of the College

Public or Private Status	Mean	Median	Minimum	Maximum
Public College	75261.36	42000.00	5.00	350000.00
Private College	76255.09	60000.00	0.00	192420.00

10.5. Mean, Median, Minimum and Maximum Library Spending on Books, 2006 (in $)

	Mean	Median	Minimum	Maximum
All Libraries	81079.47	53000.00	2000.00	425000.00

10.6. Mean, Median, Minimum and Maximum Library Spending on Books, 2006 (in $), Broken Out by College Enrollment

Number of Enrolled Students (FTE)	Mean	Median	Minimum	Maximum
Less than 1,650	34567.25	21000.00	4000.00	90000.00
1650 -- 4,000	100493.09	87000.00	26680.00	208226.00
Greater than 4,000	137275.88	79000.00	5.00	425000.00

10.7. Mean, Median, Minimum and Maximum Library Spending on Books, 2006 (in $), Broken Out by Type of College

Type of College	Mean	Median	Minimum	Maximum
Community College	16857.14	13000.00	4000.00	42000.00
4-Year or Master's Level	72487.83	48000.00	5.00	300000.00
PHD & Research University	133392.60	93500.00	2000.00	425000.00

10.8. Mean, Median, Minimum and Maximum Library Spending on Books, 2006 (in $), Broken Out by Public or Private Status of the College

Public or Private Status	Mean	Median	Minimum	Maximum
Public College	91116.45	31276.00	5.00	425000.00
Private College	73101.08	61000.00	4000.00	208226.00

10.9. Mean, Median, Minimum and Maximum Library Spending on Books, 2007 (in $)

	Mean	Median	Minimum	Maximum
All Libraries	80089.97	53684.50	2000.00	425000.00

10.10. Mean, Median, Minimum and Maximum Library Spending on Books, 2007 (in $), Broken Out by College Enrollment

Number of Enrolled Students (FTE)	Mean	Median	Minimum	Maximum
Less than 1,650	36326.56	22000.00	8000.00	90000.00
1650 -- 4,000	106712.18	90000.00	25000.00	210000.00
Greater than 4,000	121000.63	78500.00	5.00	425000.00

10.11. Mean, Median, Minimum and Maximum Library Spending on Books, 2007 (in $), Broken Out by Type of College

Type of College	Mean	Median	Minimum	Maximum
Community College	18000.00	15000.00	8000.00	42000.00
4-Year or Master's Level	65836.89	50184.50	5.00	210000.00
PHD & Research University	141200.00	95000.00	2000.00	425000.00

10.12. Mean, Median, Minimum and Maximum Library Spending on Books, 2007 (in $), Broken Out by Public or Private Status of the College

Public or Private Status	Mean	Median	Minimum	Maximum
Public College	79636.82	30000.00	5.00	425000.00
Private College	76960.79	62500.00	8000.00	210000.00

10.13. Mean, Median, Minimum and Maximum Library Spending on Electronic Books, 2005 (in $)

	Mean	Median	Minimum	Maximum
All Libraries	6691.97	720.50	0.00	97000.00

10.14. Mean, Median, Minimum and Maximum Library Spending on Electronic Books, 2005 (in $), Broken Out by College Enrollment

Number of Enrolled Students (FTE)	Mean	Median	Minimum	Maximum
Less than 1,650	7296.88	0.00	0.00	97000.00
1650 -- 4,000	829.40	497.00	0.00	2100.00
Greater than 4,000	11908.25	6593.00	0.00	50000.00

10.15. Mean, Median, Minimum and Maximum Library Spending on Electronic Books, 2005 (in $), Broken Out by Type of College

Type of College	Mean	Median	Minimum	Maximum
Community College	2642.86	0.00	0.00	15000.00
4-Year or Master's Level	7533.72	720.50	0.00	97000.00
PHD & Research University	7350.00	1000.00	0.00	50000.00

10.16. Mean, Median, Minimum and Maximum Library Spending on Electronic Books, 2005 (in $), Broken Out by Public or Private Status of the College

Public or Private Status	Mean	Median	Minimum	Maximum
Public College	8569.64	1500.00	0.00	50000.00
Private College	5555.88	223.50	0.00	97000.00

10.17. Mean, Median, Minimum and Maximum Library Spending on Electronic Books, 2006 (in $)

	Mean	Median	Minimum	Maximum
All Libraries	7370.26	1100.00	0.00	90000.00

10.18. Mean, Median, Minimum and Maximum Library Spending on Electronic Books, 2006 (in $), Broken Out by College Enrollment

Number of Enrolled Students (FTE)	Mean	Median	Minimum	Maximum
Less than 1,650	7379.53	1100.00	0.00	90000.00
1650 -- 4,000	1259.30	1096.50	0.00	4000.00
Greater than 4,000	14078.00	5272.00	0.00	50000.00

10.19. Mean, Median, Minimum and Maximum Library Spending on Electronic Books, 2006 (in $), Broken Out by Type of College

Type of College	Mean	Median	Minimum	Maximum
Community College	4985.71	2000.00	1100.00	20000.00
4-Year or Master's Level	6903.83	266.00	0.00	90000.00
PHD & Research University	9150.00	1250.00	0.00	50000.00

10.20. Mean, Median, Minimum and Maximum Library Spending on Electronic Books, 2006 (in $), Broken Out by Public or Private Status of the College

Public or Private Status	Mean	Median	Minimum	Maximum
Public College	10902.18	1500.00	0.00	50000.00
Private College	5447.71	500.00	0.00	90000.00

10.21. Mean, Median, Minimum and Maximum Library Spending on Electronic Books, 2007 (in $)

	Mean	Median	Minimum	Maximum
All Libraries	8705.97	1350.00	0.00	90000.00

10.22. Mean, Median, Minimum and Maximum Library Spending on Electronic Books, 2007 (in $), Broken Out by College Enrollment

Number of Enrolled Students (FTE)	Mean	Median	Minimum	Maximum
Less than 1,650	8021.00	1100.00	0.00	90000.00
1650 -- 4,000	1360.00	1250.00	0.00	4000.00
Greater than 4,000	18265.75	6273.00	0.00	75000.00

10.23. Mean, Median, Minimum and Maximum Library Spending on Electronic Books, 2007 (in $), Broken Out by Type of College

Type of College	Mean	Median	Minimum	Maximum
Community College	5328.57	1500.00	500.00	24000.00
4-Year or Master's Level	7571.28	500.00	0.00	90000.00
PHD & Research University	12250.00	2000.00	0.00	75000.00

10.24. Mean, Median, Minimum and Maximum Library Spending on Electronic Books, 2007 (in $), Broken Out by Public or Private Status of the College

Public or Private Status	Mean	Median	Minimum	Maximum
Public College	13875.09	2000.00	0.00	75000.00
Private College	5977.38	800.00	0.00	90000.00

The libraries in the sample purchased a mean of 79.1% of their books through book distributors or jobbers. Libraries from PHD granting institutions actually acquired a lower percentage of their total books through book jobbers or distributors than other types of libraries, perhaps reflecting their more eclectic and diverse needs. The median discount given by book distributors and jobbers for reference books was 15% and the mean, 12.28 %. For scholarly and professional publishers, the median discount was 15%, and the mean, 14.65%. Discounts were slightly higher for general trade books, averaging 19.17%. with a median of 16.5%.

10.25. Mean, Median, Minimum and Maximum Percentage of Total Book Purchases Made Though Book Distributor or Wholesaler

	Mean	Median	Minimum	Maximum
All Libraries	79.10	90.00	10.00	100.00

10.26. Mean, Median, Minimum and Maximum Percentage of Total Book Purchases Made Though Book Distributor or Wholesaler, Broken Out by College Enrollment

Number of Enrolled Students (FTE)	Mean	Median	Minimum	Maximum
Less than 1,650	73.59	90.00	0.80	100.00
1650 – 4,000	74.74	90.00	0.85	98.00
Greater than 4,000	69.53	85.00	0.75	100.00

10.27. Mean, Median, Minimum and Maximum Percentage of Total Book Purchases Made Though Book Distributor or Wholesaler, Broken Out by Type of College

Type of College	Mean	Median	Minimum	Maximum
Community College	78.69	90.00	0.80	100.00
4-Year or Master's Level	78.22	90.00	0.85	100.00
PHD & Research University	59.43	70.00	0.75	90.00

10.28. Mean, Median, Minimum and Maximum Percentage of Total Book Purchases Made Though Book Distributor or Wholesaler, Broken Out by Public or Private Status of the College

Public or Private Status	Mean	Median	Minimum	Maximum
Public College	69.30	90.00	0.75	100.00
Private College	74.65	90.00	0.85	100.00

10.29. Mean, Median, Minimum and Maximum Approximate Percentage Discount from List Price Given by Distributors for Reference Books

	Mean	Median	Minimum	Maximum
All Libraries	12.28	15.00	0.00	20.00

10.30. Mean, Median, Minimum and Maximum Approximate Percentage Discount from List Price Given by Distributors for Reference Books, Broken Out by College Enrollment

Number of Enrolled Students (FTE)	Mean	Median	Minimum	Maximum
Less than 1,650	12.91	13.00	5.00	20.00
1650 – 4,000	10.52	15.00	0.00	15.00
Greater than 4,000	9.02	10.00	0.15	18.00

10.31. Mean, Median, Minimum and Maximum Approximate Percentage Discount from List Price Given by Distributors for Reference Books, Broken Out by Type of College

Type of College	Mean	Median	Minimum	Maximum
Community College	10.83	10.00	5.00	15.00
4-Year or Master's Level	10.98	10.00	0.00	20.00
PHD & Research University	12.89	15.00	0.15	18.00

10.32. Mean, Median, Minimum and Maximum Approximate Percentage Discount from Distributors for Reference Books, Broken Out by Public or Private Status of the College

Public or Private Status	Mean	Median	Minimum	Maximum
Public College	8.82	10.00	0.15	18.00
Private College	12.49	15.00	0.00	20.00

10.33. Mean, Median, Minimum and Maximum Approximate Percentage Discount Off List Price From Distributors for Books from Scholarly and Professional Publishers

	Mean	Median	Minimum	Maximum
All Libraries	14.65	15.00	5.00	40.00

10.34. Mean, Median, Minimum and Maximum Approximate Percentage Discount Off List Price From Distributors for Books from Scholarly and Professional Publishers, Broken Out by College Enrollment

Number of Enrolled Students (FTE)	Mean	Median	Minimum	Maximum
Less than 1,650	14.79	15.00	5.00	40.00
1650 -- 4,000	15.22	15.00	10.00	20.00
Greater than 4,000	10.04	12.00	0.25	18.00

10.35. Mean, Median, Minimum and Maximum Approximate Percentage Discount Off List Price From Distributors for Books from Scholarly and Professional Publishers, Broken Out by Type of College

Type of College	Mean	Median	Minimum	Maximum
Community College	10.33	10.00	5.00	15.00
4-Year or Master's Level	14.92	15.00	5.00	40.00
PHD & Research University	14.16	15.00	0.25	20.00

10.36. Mean, Median, Minimum and Maximum Approximate Percentage Discount Off List Price From Distributors for Books from Scholarly and Professional Publishers, Broken Out by Public or Private Status of the College

Public or Private Status	Mean	Median	Minimum	Maximum
Public College	9.53	10.00	0.25	18.00
Private College	15.80	15.00	5.00	40.00

10.37. Mean, Median, Minimum and Maximum Approximate Percentage Discount Off List Price From Distributors for Books from General Trade Publishers

	Mean	Median	Minimum	Maximum
All Libraries	19.17	16.50	0.00	40.00

10.38. Mean, Median, Minimum and Maximum Approximate Percentage Discount Off List Price From Distributors for Books from General Trade Publishers, Broken Out by College Enrollment

Number of Enrolled Students (FTE)	Mean	Median	Minimum	Maximum
Less than 1,650	18.74	18.25	0.00	40.00
1650 -- 4,000	15.79	15.00	0.10	35.00
Greater than 4,000	13.54	10.00	0.25	38.00

10.39. Mean, Median, Minimum and Maximum Approximate Percentage Discount Off List Price From Distributors for Books from General Trade Publishers, Broken Out by Type of College

Type of College	Mean	Median	Minimum	Maximum
Community College	22.67	30.00	0.33	40.00
4-Year or Master's Level	15.37	15.00	0.00	40.00
PHD & Research University	16.66	15.00	0.25	38.00

10.40. Mean, Median, Minimum and Maximum Approximate Percentage Discount Off List Price From Distributors for Books from General Trade Publishers, Broken Out by Public or Private Status of the College

Public or Private Status	Mean	Median	Minimum	Maximum
Public College	19.92	18.00	0.25	40.00
Private College	15.63	15.00	0.00	40.00

11. CHAPTER ELEVEN: LAP TOP COMPUTER LENDING PROGRAMS

About 34.9% of the libraries in the sample have lap top lending programs for students. Of those libraries that do not currently have such a program, only 3.85% say that they have firm plans to start one within the next two years, but close to 20% say that they might possibly start such a program within this time frame. It is mostly the middle sized and larger colleges that are still sitting on the fence on this issue.

The libraries that have laptop lending programs have a mean stock of 12.8 laptops.

Only one program allowed its students to take the laptops home overnight. The actual number of laptops out on loan in a given day sometimes exceeded the stock of laptops since some programs would lend out the same laptop more than once a day.

11.1. Percentage of Libraries that Lend Out Laptop Computers to Students

	Yes	No
All Libraries	34.88%	65.12%

11.2. Percentage of Libraries that Lend Out Laptop Computers to Students, Broken Out by College Enrollment

Number of Enrolled Students (FTE)	Yes	No
Less than 1,650	31.58%	68.42%
1650 -- 4,000	35.71%	64.29%
Greater than 4,000	40.00%	60.00%

11.3. Percentage of Libraries that Lend Out Laptop Computers to Students, Broken Out by Type of College

Type of College	Yes	No
Community College	14.29%	85.71%
4-Year or Master's Level	39.13%	60.87%
PHD & Research University	38.46%	61.54%

11.4. Percentage of Libraries that Lend Out Laptop Computers to Students, Broken Out by Public or Private Status of the College

Public or Private Status	Yes	No
Public College	37.50%	62.50%
Private College	33.33%	66.67%

11.5. Percentage of Libraries that Currently Do Not Lend out Laptops to Students that Plan to Develop Such a Program Within the Next Two Years

	Yes	No	Possible
All Libraries	3.85%	76.92%	19.23%

11.6. Percentage of Libraries that Currently Do Not Lend out Laptops to Students that Plan to Develop Such a Program Within the Next Two Years, Broken Out by College Enrollment

Number of Enrolled Students (FTE)	Yes	No	Possible
Less than 1,650	7.69%	92.31%	0.00%
1650 -- 4,000	0.00%	50.00%	50.00%
Greater than 4,000	0.00%	80.00%	20.00%

11.7. Percentage of Libraries that Currently Do Not Lend out Laptops to Students that Plan to Develop Such a Program Within the Next Two Years, Broken Out by Type of College

Type of College	Yes	No	Possible
Community College	0.00%	100.00%	0.00%
4-Year or Master's Level	7.69%	76.92%	15.38%
PHD & Research University	0.00%	57.14%	42.86%

11.8. Percentage of Libraries that Currently Do Not Lend out Laptops to Students that Plan to Develop Such a Program Within the Next Two Years, Broken Out by Public or Private Status of the College

Public or Private Status	Yes	No	Possible
Public College	0.00%	75.00%	25.00%
Private College	5.56%	77.78%	16.67%

11.9. Mean, Median, Minimum and Maximum Stock of Laptops Available for Loan from Colleges that have Such a Lending Program

	Mean	**Median**	**Minimum**	**Maximum**
All Libraries	12.80	5.50	0.00	100.00

11.10. Mean, Median, Minimum and Maximum Stock of Laptops Available for Loan from Colleges that have Such a Lending Program, Broken Out by College Enrollment

Number of Enrolled Students (FTE)	Mean	Median	Minimum	Maximum
Less than 1,650	12.71	14.00	2.00	30.00
1650 -- 4,000	19.43	6.00	0.00	100.00
Greater than 4,000	6.20	5.00	0.00	15.00

11.11. Mean, Median, Minimum and Maximum Stock of Laptops Available for Loan from Colleges that have Such a Lending Program, Broken Out by Type of College

Type of College	Mean	Median	Minimum	Maximum
Community College	5.00	5.00	5.00	5.00
4-Year or Master's Level	16.80	8.00	0.00	100.00
PHD & Research University	10.38	7.50	0.00	30.00

11.12. Mean, Median, Minimum and Maximum Stock of Laptops Available for Loan from Colleges that have Such a Lending Program, Broken Out by Public or Private Status of the College

Public or Private Status	Mean	Median	Minimum	Maximum
Public College	7.00	5.00	0.00	20.00
Private College	18.18	10.00	0.00	100.00

11.13. Percentage of Libraries with Laptop Lending Programs that Allow Students to Take Home Laptops Overnight

	Yes	No
All Libraries	4.17%	95.83%

11.14. Percentage of Libraries with Laptop Lending Programs that Allow Students to Take Home Laptops Overnight, Broken Out by College Enrollment

Number of Enrolled Students (FTE)	Yes	No
Less than 1,650	9.09%	90.91%
1650 -- 4,000	0.00%	100.00%
Greater than 4,000	0.00%	100.00%

11.15. Percentage of Libraries with Laptop Lending Programs that Allow Students to Take Home Laptops Overnight, Broken Out by Type of College

Type of College	Yes	No
Community College	0.00%	100.00%
4-Year or Master's Level	7.14%	92.86%
PHD & Research University	0.00%	100.00%

11.16. Percentage of Libraries with Laptop Lending Programs that Allow Students to Take Home Laptops Overnight, Broken Out by Public or Private Status of the College

Public or Private Status	Yes	No
Public College	0.00%	100.00%
Private College	7.14%	92.86%

11.17. Mean, Median, Minimum and Maximum Number of Laptops Out on Loan on a Typical Day

	Mean	Median	Minimum	Maximum
All Libraries	14.06	7.50	0.00	110.00

11.18. Mean, Median, Minimum and Maximum Number of Laptops Out on Loan on a Typical Day, Broken Out by College Enrollment

Number of Enrolled Students (FTE)	Mean	Median	Minimum	Maximum
Less than 1,650	6.29	3.00	0.00	14.00
1650 -- 4,000	32.00	9.00	0.00	110.00
Greater than 4,000	10.60	9.00	1.00	30.00

11.19. Mean, Median, Minimum and Maximum Number of Laptops Out on Loan on a Typical Day, Broken Out by Type of College

Type of College	Mean	Median	Minimum	Maximum
Community College	2.00	2.00	2.00	2.00
4-Year or Master's Level	20.00	9.50	0.00	110.00
PHD & Research University	9.00	3.00	0.00	30.00

11.20. Mean, Median, Minimum and Maximum Number of Laptops Out on Loan on a Typical Day, Broken Out by Public or Private Status of the College

Public or Private Status	Mean	Median	Minimum	Maximum
Public College	8.29	3.00	1.00	30.00
Private College	18.56	10.00	0.00	110.00

12. CHAPTER TWELVE: JOURNALS & OTHER PERIODICALS

Spending on journals in both print and electronic formats was a mean of $214,507 in 2005, and rose to $227,800, an increase of 6.2%, a relatively low increase by historic standards, but high relative to other mediums. The libraries in the sample expected to increase mean spending to $239,294 in 2007, an increase of 5.05%, once again, low by historic standards for this medium.

Spending on periodicals other than journals rose to a mean of $58,056 in 2006 from $56,496 in 2005, an increase of 2.76%. The libraries in the sample expect to increase spending on non-journal periodicals to a mean of $59,289 in 2007, an increase of 2.12%.

12.1. Mean, Median, Minimum and Maximum Spending on Subscriptions to Print and Electronic Versions of Scholarly Journals, 2005 (in $)

	Mean	Median	Minimum	Maximum
All Libraries	214507.38	98983.00	2500.00	1500000.00

12.2. Mean, Median, Minimum and Maximum Spending on Subscriptions to Print and Electronic Versions of Scholarly Journals, 2005 (in $), Broken Out by College Enrollment

Number of Enrolled Students (FTE)	Mean	Median	Minimum	Maximum
Less than 1,650	58386.00	67500.00	2500.00	119381.00
1650 -- 4,000	147629.86	125000.00	18000.00	276000.00
Greater than 4,000	708854.83	663210.00	137000.00	1500000.00

12.3. Mean, Median, Minimum and Maximum Spending on Subscriptions to Print and Electronic Versions of Scholarly Journals, 2005 (in $), Broken Out by Type of College

Type of College	Mean	Median	Minimum	Maximum
Community College	9883.33	9250.00	2500.00	18000.00
4-Year or Master's Level	175980.33	95000.00	51210.00	750000.00
PHD & Research University	440213.63	206500.00	101000.00	1500000.00

12.4. Mean, Median, Minimum and Maximum Spending on Subscriptions to Print and Electronic Versions of Scholarly Journals, 2005 (in $), Broken Out by Public or Private Status of the College

Public or Private Status	Mean	Median	Minimum	Maximum
Public College	442133.63	337074.50	8500.00	1500000.00
Private College	127792.62	95000.00	2500.00	752560.00

12.5. Mean, Median, Minimum and Maximum Spending on Subscriptions to Print and Electronic Versions of Scholarly Journals, 2006 (in $)

	Mean	Median	Minimum	Maximum
All Libraries	227800.38	104000.00	3255.00	1700000.00

12.6. Mean, Median, Minimum and Maximum Spending on Subscriptions to Print and Electronic Versions of Scholarly Journals, 2006 (in $), Broken Out by College Enrollment

Number of Enrolled Students (FTE)	Mean	Median	Minimum	Maximum
Less than 1,650	59773.06	68500.00	3255.00	128000.00
1650 -- 4,000	164308.29	139000.00	18000.00	295000.00
Greater than 4,000	749947.33	678842.00	142000.00	1700000.00

12.7. Mean, Median, Minimum and Maximum Spending on Subscriptions to Print and Electronic Versions of Scholarly Journals, 2006 (in $), Broken Out by Type of College

Type of College	Mean	Median	Minimum	Maximum
Community College	11309.17	11650.00	3255.00	18000.00
4-Year or Master's Level	184882.13	93000.00	54004.00	750000.00
PHD & Research University	470640.50	218500.00	104000.00	1700000.00

12.8. Mean, Median, Minimum and Maximum Spending on Subscriptions to Print and Electronic Versions of Scholarly Journals, 2006 (in $), Broken Out by Public or Private Status of the College

Public or Private Status	Mean	Median	Minimum	Maximum
Public College	473982.50	346000.00	8300.00	1700000.00
Private College	134016.71	93000.00	3255.00	749124.00

12.9. Mean, Median, Minimum and Maximum Spending on Subscriptions to Print and Electronic Versions of Scholarly Journals, 2007 (in $)

	Mean	Median	Minimum	Maximum
All Libraries	239293.66	107000.00	3450.00	1850000.00

12.10. Mean, Median, Minimum and Maximum Spending on Subscriptions to Print and Electronic Versions of Scholarly Journals, 2007 (in $), Broken Out by College Enrollment

Number of Enrolled Students (FTE)	Mean	Median	Minimum	Maximum
Less than 1,650	60395.06	70000.00	3450.00	125000.00
1650 -- 4,000	171823.86	144000.00	18000.00	295000.00
Greater than 4,000	795071.33	689214.00	142000.00	1850000.00

12.11. Mean, Median, Minimum and Maximum Spending on Subscriptions to Print and Electronic Versions of Scholarly Journals, 2007 (in $), Broken Out by Type of College

Type of College	Mean	Median	Minimum	Maximum
Community College	13225.00	14500.00	3450.00	20000.00
4-Year or Master's Level	191811.07	91000.00	53721.00	800000.00
PHD & Research University	497875.00	218500.00	107000.00	1850000.00

12.12. Mean, Median, Minimum and Maximum Spending on Subscriptions to Print and Electronic Versions of Scholarly Journals, 2007 (in $), Broken Out by Public or Private Status of the College

Public or Private Status	Mean	Median	Minimum	Maximum
Public College	508041.00	371000.00	8900.00	1850000.00
Private College	136913.71	91000.00	3450.00	750000.00

12.13. Mean, Median, Minimum and Maximum Spending on Print Versions of Periodicals that are not Journals, 2005 (in $)

	Mean	Median	Minimum	Maximum
All Libraries	56496.41	3000.00	0.00	685000.00

12.14. Mean, Median, Minimum and Maximum Spending on Print Versions of Periodicals that are not Journals, 2005 (in $), Broken Out by College Enrollment

Number of Enrolled Students (FTE)	Mean	Median	Minimum	Maximum
Less than 1,650	8609.47	615.00	0.00	62000.00
1650 – 4,000	23995.52	2000.00	0.10	135447.00
Greater than 4,000	208714.67	142144.00	10000.00	685000.00

12.15. Mean, Median, Minimum and Maximum Spending on Print Versions of Periodicals that are not Journals, 2005 (in $), Broken Out by Type of College

Type of College	Mean	Median	Minimum	Maximum
Community College	3168.57	250.00	0.00	17000.00
4-Year or Master's Level	27843.54	5747.00	0.00	135447.00
PHD & Research University	163036.73	23000.00	0.00	685000.00

12.16. Mean, Median, Minimum and Maximum Spending on Print Versions of Periodicals that are not Journals, 2005 (in $), Broken Out by Public or Private Status of the College

Public or Private Status	Mean	Median	Minimum	Maximum
Public College	121281.22	17000.00	0.00	685000.00
Private College	24104.01	1100.00	0.00	182257.00

12.17. Mean, Median, Minimum and Maximum Spending on Print Versions of Periodicals that are not Journals, 2006 (in $)

	Mean	Median	Minimum	Maximum
All Libraries	58055.89	3000.00	0.00	695000.00

12.18. Mean, Median, Minimum and Maximum Spending on Print Versions of Periodicals that are not Journals, 2006 (in $), Broken Out by College Enrollment

Number of Enrolled Students (FTE)	Mean	Median	Minimum	Maximum
Less than 1,650	7811.67	1000.00	0.00	56000.00
1650 – 4,000	25618.35	2000.00	0.10	145154.00
Greater than 4,000	216104.00	146812.00	10000.00	695000.00

12.19. Mean, Median, Minimum and Maximum Spending on Print Versions of Periodicals that are not Journals, 2006 (in $), Broken Out by Type of College

Type of College	Mean	Median	Minimum	Maximum
Community College	3157.14	500.00	0.00	16000.00
4-Year or Master's Level	28619.92	6000.00	0.00	145154.00
PHD & Research University	167621.44	23000.00	0.00	695000.00

12.20. Mean, Median, Minimum and Maximum Spending on Print Versions of Periodicals that are not Journals, 2006 (in $), Broken Out by Public or Private Status of the College

Public or Private Status	Mean	Median	Minimum	Maximum
Public College	126419.33	16000.00	0.00	695000.00
Private College	23874.17	1150.00	0.00	179350.00

12.21. Mean, Median, Minimum and Maximum Spending on Print Versions of Periodicals that are not Journals, 2007 (in $)

	Mean	Median	Minimum	Maximum
All Libraries	59289.48	3000.00	0.00	700000.00

12.22. Mean, Median, Minimum and Maximum Spending on Print Versions of Periodicals that are not Journals, 2007 (in $), Broken Out by College Enrollment

Number of Enrolled Students (FTE)	Mean	Median	Minimum	Maximum
Less than 1,650	7484.93	1000.00	0.00	51000.00
1650 – 4,000	24759.33	2000.00	0.00	140000.00
Greater than 4,000	223331.00	153993.00	10000.00	700000.00

12.23. Mean, Median, Minimum and Maximum Spending on Print Versions of Periodicals that are not Journals, 2007 (in $), Broken Out by Type of College

Type of College	Mean	Median	Minimum	Maximum
Community College	3245.71	500.00	0.00	16000.00
4-Year or Master's Level	28853.54	6000.00	0.00	140000.00
PHD & Research University	171857.14	22000.00	0.00	700000.00

12.24. Mean, Median, Minimum and Maximum Spending on Print Versions of Periodicals that are not Journals, 2007 (in $), Broken Out by Public or Private Status of the College

Public or Private Status	Mean	Median	Minimum	Maximum
Public College	131165.11	16000.00	0.00	700000.00
Private College	23351.67	1200.00	0.00	180000.00

13. CHAPTER THIRTEEN: DIGITAL DEPOSITORIES

Only 2.44% of the libraries in the sample maintained a digital depository for works by their own faculty members and all that maintained depositories were PHD-granting institutions. A bit more than 10% of the colleges in the sample plan to develop a digital depository within the next two years and a further third say that developing one is a possibility.

13.1. Percentage of Libraries that Maintain a Digital Depository

	Yes	No
All Libraries	2.44%	97.56%

13.2. Percentage of Libraries that Maintain a Digital Depository, Broken Out by College Enrollment

Number of Enrolled Students (FTE)	Yes	No
Less than 1,650	0.00%	100.00%
1650 -- 4,000	0.00%	100.00%
Greater than 4,000	10.00%	90.00%

13.3. Percentage of Libraries that Maintain a Digital Depository, Broken Out by Type of College

Type of College	Yes	No
Community College	0.00%	100.00%
4-Year or Master's Level	0.00%	100.00%
PHD & Research University	8.33%	91.67%

13.4. Percentage of Libraries that Maintain a Digital Depository, Broken Out by Public or Private Status of the College

Public or Private Status	Yes	No
Public College	7.14%	92.86%
Private College	0.00%	100.00%

13.5. Percentage of Libraries that Plan to Implement a Digital Depository Within Two Years

	Yes	No	Perhaps
All Libraries	10.26%	56.41%	33.33%

13.6. Percentage of Libraries that Plan to Implement a Digital Depository Within Two Years, Broken Out by College Enrollment

Number of Enrolled Students (FTE)	Yes	No	Perhaps
Less than 1,650	11.11%	61.11%	27.78%
1650 -- 4,000	8.33%	41.67%	50.00%
Greater than 4,000	11.11%	66.67%	22.22%

13.7. Percentage of Libraries that Plan to Implement a Digital Depository Within Two Years, Broken Out by Type of College

Type of College	Yes	No	Perhaps
Community College	0.00%	71.43%	28.57%
4-Year or Master's Level	19.05%	52.38%	28.57%
PHD & Research University	0.00%	54.55%	45.45%

13.8. Percentage of Libraries that Plan to Implement a Digital Depository Within Two Years, Broken Out by Public or Private Status of the College

Public or Private Status	Yes	No	Perhaps
Public College	8.33%	83.33%	8.33%
Private College	11.11%	44.44%	44.44%

13.9. Percentage of Libraries that Use Software that Links Catalog References to Full Text of E-Collections of Journals or Other Periodicals

	Yes	No
All Libraries	53.66%	46.34%

13.10. Percentage of Libraries that Use Software that Links Catalog References to Full Text of E-Collections of Journals or Other Periodicals, Broken Out by College Enrollment

Number of Enrolled Students (FTE)	Yes	No
Less than 1,650	38.89%	61.11%
1650 -- 4,000	46.15%	53.85%
Greater than 4,000	90.00%	10.00%

13.11. Percentage of Libraries that Use Software that Links Catalog References to Full Text of E-Collections of Journals or Other Periodicals, Broken Out by Type of College

Type of College	Yes	No
Community College	0.00%	100.00%
4-Year or Master's Level	63.64%	36.36%
PHD & Research University	66.67%	33.33%

13.12. Percentage of Libraries that Use Software that Links Catalog References to Full Text of E-Collections of Journals or Other Periodicals, Broken Out by Public or Private Status of the College

Public or Private Status	Yes	No
Public College	64.29%	35.71%
Private College	48.15%	51.85%

13.13. Percentage of Libraries that Use RSS Feeds to Download Pre-Selected Tables of Contents to Journals to Send to Patrons or to Use for Library Research

	Yes	No
All Libraries	10.00%	90.00%

13.14. Percentage of Libraries that Use RSS Feeds to Download Pre-Selected Tables of Contents to Journals to Send to Patrons or to Use for Library Research, Broken Out by College Enrollment

Number of Enrolled Students (FTE)	Yes	No
Less than 1,650	11.11%	88.89%
1650 -- 4,000	0.00%	100.00%
Greater than 4,000	20.00%	80.00%

13.15. Percentage of Libraries that Use RSS Feeds to Download Pre-Selected Tables of Contents to Journals to Send to Patrons or to Use for Library Research, Broken Out by Type of College

Type of College	Yes	No
Community College	0.00%	100.00%
4-Year or Master's Level	19.05%	80.95%
PHD & Research University	0.00%	100.00%

13.16. Percentage of Libraries that Use RSS Feeds to Download Pre-Selected Tables of Contents to Journals to Send to Patrons or to Use for Library Research, Broken Out by Public or Private Status of the College

Public or Private Status	Yes	No
Public College	14.29%	85.71%
Private College	7.69%	92.31%

14. CHAPTER FOURTEEN: LIBRARIAN PATRON EDUCATION WORK LOAD

Almost 37% of the libraries in the sample spend about 10% of total librarian staff time conducting classes, seminars and formal tutorials for students and faculty. A slightly lower percentage – 34.15% -- spend between 10% and 20% of their staff time on these pursuits. Nearly a quarter of the libraries in the sample spend between 20% and 35% of librarians staff time in teaching, while 4.88% spend from 35% to 50% of their time doing so. The amount of time spent teaching did not seem to vary considerably by type or size of college. However, public colleges spend far more staff time in teaching than private college libraries, perhaps reflecting the 'digital divide" and a possibly lower level or preparation or exposure to information technology among public college students. Nonetheless, community college students whom, one would think, would be less exposed to information technology than students of more advanced colleges, did not receive significantly more instruction time than the norm. Perhaps the difference is that public colleges, especially large state universities, have made great efforts in recent years to become more conscious of information literacy concerns.

14.1. Percentage of Librarian Staff Time Spent in Conducting Classes, Seminars and Formal Tutorials for Students & Faculty

	Less than 10%	10% to 20%	20% to 35%	35% to 50%	More than 50%
All Libraries	36.59%	34.15%	24.39%	4.88%	0.00%

14.2. Percentage of Librarian Staff Time Spent in Conducting Classes, Seminars and Formal Tutorials for Students & Faculty, Broken Out by College Enrollment

Number of Enrolled Students (FTE)	Less than 10%	10% to 20%	20% to 35%	35% to 50%	More than 50%
Less than 1,650	44.44%	33.33%	22.22%	0.00%	0.00%
1650 -- 4,000	46.15%	15.38%	30.77%	7.69%	0.00%
Greater than 4,000	10.00%	60.00%	20.00%	10.00%	0.00%

14.3. Percentage of Librarian Staff Time Spent in Conducting Classes, Seminars and Formal Tutorials for Students & Faculty, Broken Out by Type of College

Type of College	Less than 10%	10% to 20%	20% to 35%	35% to 50%	More than 50%
Community College	28.57%	42.86%	28.57%	0.00%	0.00%
4-Year or Master's Level	45.45%	27.27%	22.73%	4.55%	0.00%
PHD & Research University	25.00%	41.67%	25.00%	8.33%	0.00%

14.4. Percentage of Librarian Staff Time Spent in Conducting Classes, Seminars and Formal Tutorials for Students & Faculty, Broken Out by Public or Private Status of the College

Public or Private Status	Less than 10%	10% to 20%	20% to 35%	35% to 50%	More than 50%
Public College	14.29%	42.86%	35.71%	7.14%	0.00%
Private College	48.15%	29.63%	18.52%	3.70%	0.00%

The librarians in the sample spent a mean of 8.89% of their total staff time in responding to queries from patrons located outside the library about use of the library's databases. Librarians in larger colleges, public colleges, and those offering PHD level degrees, tend to spend much more time on this function than their counterparts.

14.5. Mean, Median, Minimum and Maximum Percentage of Librarian Staff Time Spent in Responding to Queries from Patrons from Outside the Library about Use of Databases from Remote Locations

	Mean	Median	Minimum	Maximum
All Libraries	8.89	6.50	1.00	40.00

14.6. Mean, Median, Minimum and Maximum Percentage of Librarian Staff Time Spent in Responding to Queries from Patrons from Outside the Library about Use of Databases from Remote Locations, Broken Out by College Enrollment

Number of Enrolled Students (FTE)	Mean	Median	Minimum	Maximum
Less than 1,650	5.38	5.00	1.00	10.00
1650 -- 4,000	7.64	5.00	1.00	20.00
Greater than 4,000	16.67	10.00	5.00	40.00

14.7. Mean, Median, Minimum and Maximum Percentage of Librarian Staff Time Spent in Responding to Queries from Patrons from Outside the Library about Use of Databases from Remote Locations, Broken Out by Type of College

Type of College	Mean	Median	Minimum	Maximum
Community College	5.33	5.00	2.00	10.00
4-Year or Master's Level	7.22	5.00	1.00	20.00
PHD & Research University	13.17	10.00	1.00	40.00

14.8. Mean, Median, Minimum and Maximum Percentage of Librarian Staff Time Spent in Responding to Queries from Patrons from Outside the Library about Use of Databases from Remote Locations, Broken Out by Public or Private Status of the College

Public or Private Status	Mean	Median	Minimum	Maximum
Public College	14.17	10.00	5.00	40.00
Private College	6.25	5.00	1.00	20.00

More than 71% of the libraries in the sample said that their student education work load had increased over the past two years, while less than 5% said that this work load had lessened in this period.

14.9. Trend in the Library's Student Education Workload

	Increased In The Past Two Years	Stayed About The Same In The Past Two Years	Declined In The Past Two Years
All Libraries	71.43%	23.81%	4.76%

14.10.   Trend in the Library's Student Education Workload, Broken Out by College Enrollment

Number of Enrolled Students (FTE)	Increased In The Past Two Years	Stayed About The Same In The Past Two Years	Declined In The Past Two Years
Less than 1,650	66.67%	27.78%	5.56%
1650 -- 4,000	71.43%	28.57%	0.00%
Greater than 4,000	80.00%	10.00%	10.00%

14.11. Trend in the Library's Student Education Workload, Broken Out by Type of College

Type of College	Increased In The Past Two Years	Stayed About The Same In The Past Two Years	Declined In The Past Two Years
Community College	57.14%	42.86%	0.00%
4-Year or Master's Level	78.26%	17.39%	4.35%
PHD & Research University	66.67%	25.00%	8.33%

14.12. Trend in the Library's Student Education Workload, Broken Out by Public or Private Status of the College

Public or Private Status	Increased In The Past Two Years	Stayed About The Same In The Past Two Years	Declined In The Past Two Years
Public College	66.67%	26.67%	6.67%
Private College	74.07%	22.22%	3.70%

15. CHAPTER FIFTEEN: AUDIO VISUAL MATERIALS

The colleges in the sample spent a mean of $7,491 on audio visual materials in 2005, and increased spending significantly to $8,222 in 2006. Also colleges expected to significantly increase spending once again in 2007, to a mean of $8,908.

15.1. Mean, Median, Minimum and Maximum Spending on Audio-Visual Materials, 2005 (in $)

	Mean	Median	Minimum	Maximum
All Libraries	7491.47	5169.50	0.00	30000.00

15.2. Mean, Median, Minimum and Maximum Spending on Audio-Visual Materials, 2005 (in $), Broken Out by College Enrollment

Number of Enrolled Students (FTE)	Mean	Median	Minimum	Maximum
Less than 1,650	4802.65	5000.00	0.00	15861.00
1650 -- 4,000	7024.33	7583.00	0.00	15500.00
Greater than 4,000	13869.89	10000.00	0.00	30000.00

15.3. Mean, Median, Minimum and Maximum Spending on Audio-Visual Materials, 2005 (in $), Broken Out by Type of College

Type of College	Mean	Median	Minimum	Maximum
Community College	4908.71	2000.00	0.00	15861.00
4-Year or Master's Level	7586.11	5169.50	0.00	30000.00
PHD & Research University	9878.20	8100.00	0.00	29629.00

15.4. Mean, Median, Minimum and Maximum Spending on Audio-Visual Materials, 2005 (in $), Broken Out by Public or Private Status of the College

Public or Private Status	Mean	Median	Minimum	Maximum
Public College	10380.08	9100.00	0.00	30000.00
Private College	6310.09	5000.00	0.00	29629.00

15.5. Mean, Median, Minimum and Maximum Spending on Audio-Visual Materials, 2006 (in $)

	Mean	Median	Minimum	Maximum
All Libraries	8221.86	5162.50	0.00	35000.00

15.6. Mean, Median, Minimum and Maximum Spending on Audio-Visual Materials, 2006 (in $), Broken Out by College Enrollment

Number of Enrolled Students (FTE)	Mean	Median	Minimum	Maximum
Less than 1,650	4642.12	3000.00	500.00	11815.00
1650 -- 4,000	8330.11	11000.00	0.00	16000.00
Greater than 4,000	15788.89	10000.00	0.00	35000.00

15.7. Mean, Median, Minimum and Maximum Spending on Audio-Visual Materials, 2006 (in $), Broken Out by Type of College

Type of College	Mean	Median	Minimum	Maximum
Community College	4748.57	2100.00	1000.00	11815.00
4-Year or Master's Level	7823.61	4474.50	0.00	30000.00
PHD & Research University	12192.20	9250.00	0.00	35000.00

15.8. Mean, Median, Minimum and Maximum Spending on Audio-Visual Materials, 2006 (in $), Broken Out by Public or Private Status of the College

Public or Private Status	Mean	Median	Minimum	Maximum
Public College	11276.25	8750.00	0.00	35000.00
Private College	6985.74	5000.00	0.00	31600.00

15.9. Mean, Median, Minimum and Maximum Spending on Audio-Visual Materials, 2007 (in $)

	Mean	Median	Minimum	Maximum
All Libraries	8907.53	5250.00	0.00	40000.00

15.10. Mean, Median, Minimum and Maximum Spending on Audio-Visual Materials, 2007 (in $), Broken Out by College Enrollment

Number of Enrolled Students (FTE)	Mean	Median	Minimum	Maximum
Less than 1,650	5561.76	5000.00	500.00	17000.00
1650 -- 4,000	8158.88	8000.00	0.00	17000.00
Greater than 4,000	18450.00	18500.00	0.00	40000.00

15.11. Mean, Median, Minimum and Maximum Spending on Audio-Visual Materials, 2007 (in $), Broken Out by Type of College

Type of College	Mean	Median	Minimum	Maximum
Community College	6714.29	5000.00	2000.00	17000.00
4-Year or Master's Level	7588.18	3949.00	0.00	30000.00
PHD & Research University	14602.44	10000.00	0.00	40000.00

15.12. Mean, Median, Minimum and Maximum Spending on Audio-Visual Materials, 2007(in $), Broken Out by Public or Private Status of the College

Public or Private Status	Mean	Median	Minimum	Maximum
Public College	13554.55	10000.00	0.00	40000.00
Private College	7196.41	5000.00	0.00	32000.00

NOTE: FOR THE FOLLOWING TABLES ON SPECIAL COLLECTIONS THE DEFINTION OF "SPECIAL COLLECTION" IN THE QUESTIONNAIRE WAS FOR A COLLECTION THAT REQUIRED ITS OWN CURATOR OR DEDICATED LIBRARY STAFF. THIS PROVISO APPLIES TO ALL TYPES OF SPECIAL COLLECTIONS.

15.13. Percentage of Libraries that Maintain a Rare Books Special Collection

	Yes	No
All Libraries	34.00%	66.00%

15.14. Percentage of Libraries that Maintain a Rare Books Special Collection, Broken Out by College Enrollment

Number of Enrolled Students (FTE)	Yes	No
Less than 1,650	28.57%	71.43%
1650 -- 4,000	37.50%	62.50%
Greater than 4,000	38.46%	61.54%

15.15. Percentage of Libraries that Maintain a Rare Books Special Collection, Broken Out by Type of College

Type of College	Yes	No
Community College	11.11%	88.89%
4-Year or Master's Level	46.15%	53.85%
PHD & Research University	26.67%	73.33%

15.16. Percentage of Libraries that Maintain a Rare Books Special Collection, Broken Out by Public or Private Status of the College

Public or Private Status	Yes	No
Public College	25.00%	75.00%
Private College	40.00%	60.00%

15.17. Percentage of Libraries that Maintain a Special Collection of Maps or Globes

	Yes	No
All Libraries	5.88%	94.12%

15.18. Percentage of Libraries that Maintain a Special Collection of Maps or Globes, Broken Out by College Enrollment

Number of Enrolled Students (FTE)	Yes	No
Less than 1,650	0.00%	100.00%
1650 -- 4,000	6.25%	93.75%
Greater than 4,000	15.38%	84.62%

15.19. Percentage of Libraries that Maintain a Special Collection of Maps or Globes, Broken Out by Type of College

Type of College	Yes	No
Community College	0.00%	100.00%
4-Year or Master's Level	3.85%	96.15%
PHD & Research University	13.33%	86.67%

15.20. Percentage of Libraries that Maintain a Special Collection of Maps or Globes, Broken Out by Public or Private Status of the College

Public or Private Status	Yes	No
Public College	10.00%	90.00%
Private College	3.33%	96.67%

15.21. Percentage of Libraries that Maintain a Special Collection of Photographs

	Yes	No
All Libraries	25.00%	75.00%

15.22. Percentage of Libraries that Maintain a Special Collection of Photographs, Broken Out by College Enrollment

Number of Enrolled Students (FTE)	Yes	No
Less than 1,650	19.05%	80.95%
1650 – 4,000	31.25%	68.75%
Greater than 4,000	30.77%	69.23%

15.23. Percentage of Libraries that Maintain a Special Collection of Photographs, Broken Out by Type of College

Type of College	Yes	No
Community College	0.00%	100.00%
4-Year or Master's Level	34.62%	65.38%
PHD & Research University	26.67%	73.33%

15.24. Percentage of Libraries that Maintain a Special Collection of Photographs, Broken Out by Public or Private Status of the College

Public or Private Status	Yes	No
Public College	20.00%	80.00%
Private College	30.00%	70.00%

15.25. Percentage of Libraries that Maintain a Special Collection of Films

	Yes	No
All Libraries	11.54%	88.46%

15.26. Percentage of Libraries that Maintain a Special Collection of Films, Broken Out by College Enrollment

Number of Enrolled Students (FTE)	Yes	No
Less than 1,650	0.00%	100.00%
1650 – 4,000	18.75%	81.25%
Greater than 4,000	23.08%	76.92%

15.27. Percentage of Libraries that Maintain a Special Collection of Films, Broken Out by Type of College

Type of College	Yes	No
Community College	0.00%	100.00%
4-Year or Master's Level	15.38%	84.62%
PHD & Research University	13.33%	86.67%

15.28. Percentage of Libraries that Maintain a Special Collection of Films, Broken Out by Public or Private Status of the College

Public or Private Status	Yes	No
Public College	10.00%	90.00%
Private College	13.33%	86.67%

15.29. Percentage of Libraries that Maintain a Special Collection of Musical Recordings

	Yes	No
All Libraries	11.54%	88.46%

15.30. Percentage of Libraries that Maintain a Special Collection of Musical Recordings, Broken Out by College Enrollment

Number of Enrolled Students (FTE)	Yes	No
Less than 1,650	4.76%	95.24%
1650 – 4,000	18.75%	81.25%
Greater than 4,000	15.38%	84.62%

15.31. Percentage of Libraries that Maintain a Special Collection of Musical Recordings, Broken Out by Type of College

Type of College	Yes	No
Community College	0.00%	100.00%
4-Year or Master's Level	15.38%	84.62%
PHD & Research University	13.33%	86.67%

15.32. Percentage of Libraries that Maintain a Special Collection of Musical Recordings, Broken Out by Public or Private Status of the College

Public or Private Status	Yes	No
Public College	5.00%	95.00%
Private College	16.67%	83.33%

15.33. Percentage of Libraries that Maintain a Special Collection of Digital Images

	Yes	No
All Libraries	15.38%	84.62%

15.34. Percentage of Libraries that Maintain a Special Collection of Digital Images, Broken Out by College Enrollment

Number of Enrolled Students (FTE)	Yes	No
Less than 1,650	4.76%	95.24%
1650 – 4,000	25.00%	75.00%
Greater than 4,000	23.08%	76.92%

15.35. Percentage of Libraries that Maintain a Special Collection of Digital Images, Broken Out by Type of College

Type of College	Yes	No
Community College	0.00%	100.00%
4-Year or Master's Level	23.08%	76.92%
PHD & Research University	13.33%	86.67%

15.36. Percentage of Libraries that Maintain a Special Collection of Digital Images, Broken Out by Public or Private Status of the College

Public or Private Status	Yes	No
Public College	15.00%	85.00%
Private College	16.67%	83.33%

15.37. Percentage of Libraries that Maintain a Special Collection of Artwork or Prints

	Yes	No
All Libraries	9.62%	90.38%

15.38. Percentage of Libraries that Maintain a Special Collection of Artwork or Prints, Broken Out by College Enrollment

Number of Enrolled Students (FTE)	Yes	No
Less than 1,650	4.76%	95.24%
1650 – 4,000	12.50%	87.50%
Greater than 4,000	15.38%	84.62%

15.39. Percentage of Libraries that Maintain a Special Collection of Artwork or Prints, Broken Out by Type of College

Type of College	Yes	No
Community College	0.00%	100.00%
4-Year or Master's Level	15.38%	84.62%
PHD & Research University	6.67%	93.33%

15.40. Percentage of Libraries that Maintain a Special Collection of Artwork or Prints, Broken Out by Public or Private Status of the College

Public or Private Status	Yes	No
Public College	10.00%	90.00%
Private College	10.00%	90.00%

15.41. Percentage of Libraries that Maintain a Special Collection in Numanistics

	Yes	No
All Libraries	0.00%	98.08%

15.42. Percentage of Libraries that Maintain a Special Collection in Numanistics, Broken Out by College Enrollment

Number of Enrolled Students (FTE)	Yes	No
Less than 1,650	0.00%	100.00%
1650 -- 4,000	0.00%	100.00%
Greater than 4,000	0.00%	100.00%

15.43. Percentage of Libraries that Maintain a Special Collection in Numanistics, Broken Out by Type of College

Type of College	Yes	No
Community College	0.00%	100.00%
4-Year or Master's Level	0.00%	100.00%
PHD & Research University	0.00%	100.00%

15.44. Percentage of Libraries that Maintain a Special Collection in Numanistics, Broken Out by Public or Private Status of the College

Public or Private Status	Yes	No
Public College	0.00%	100.00%
Private College	0.00%	100.00%

16. CHAPTER SIXTEEN: CATALOGING

The college libraries in the sample spent a mean of $20,493 on their cataloging department budget, or its equivalent, if they had no such department. Libraries spent little on outsourced cataloging, with mean spending of just $591. Most libraries spent nothing on outsourced cataloging.

More than half of the libraries in the sample now catalog web resources, and even more than 57% of community colleges do so. Close to 32% of the libraries in the sample make archival and finding aids available on the web.

16.1. Mean, Median, Minimum and Maximum Cataloging Department Budget (in $)

	Mean	Median	Minimum	Maximum
All Libraries	20492.92	7500.00	0.00	90000.00

16.2. Mean, Median, Minimum and Maximum Cataloging Department Budget (in $), Broken Out by College Enrollment

Number of Enrolled Students (FTE)	Mean	Median	Minimum	Maximum
Less than 1,650	10828.64	5000.00	655.00	60000.00
1650 -- 4,000	30370.10	25000.00	3085.00	70000.00
Greater than 4,000	27500.00	10000.00	0.00	90000.00

16.3. Mean, Median, Minimum and Maximum Cataloging Department Budget (in $), Broken Out by Type of College

Type of College	Mean	Median	Minimum	Maximum
Community College	6000.00	5000.00	1000.00	15000.00
4-Year or Master's Level	17921.07	7000.00	0.00	67883.00
PHD & Research University	46800.00	29000.00	20000.00	90000.00

16.4. Mean, Median, Minimum and Maximum Cataloging Department Budget (in $), Broken Out by Public or Private Status of the College

Public or Private Status	Mean	Median	Minimum	Maximum
Public College	14125.00	3500.00	0.00	90000.00
Private College	24695.06	15000.00	655.00	70000.00

16.5. Mean, Median, Minimum and Maximum Spending for Outsourced Cataloging (in $)

	Mean	Median	Minimum	Maximum
All Libraries	590.91	0.00	0.00	20000.00

16.6. Mean, Median, Minimum and Maximum Spending for Outsourced Cataloging (in $), Broken Out by College Enrollment

Number of Enrolled Students (FTE)	Mean	Median	Minimum	Maximum
Less than 1,650	58.82	0.00	0.00	1000.00
1650 -- 4,000	454.55	0.00	0.00	5000.00
Greater than 4,000	3333.33	0.00	0.00	20000.00

16.7. Mean, Median, Minimum and Maximum Spending for Outsourced Cataloging (in $), Broken Out by Type of College

Type of College	Mean	Median	Minimum	Maximum
Community College	142.86	0.00	0.00	1000.00
4-Year or Master's Level	0.00	0.00	0.00	0.00
PHD & Research University	2777.78	0.00	0.00	20000.00

16.8. Mean, Median, Minimum and Maximum Spending for Outsourced Cataloging (in $), Broken Out by Public or Private Status of the College

Public or Private Status	Mean	Median	Minimum	Maximum
Public College	100.00	0.00	0.00	1000.00
Private College	1041.67	0.00	0.00	20000.00

16.9. Percentage of Libraries that Catalog Web Resources

	Yes	No
All Libraries	53.66%	46.34%

16.10. Percentage of Libraries that Catalog Web Resources, Broken Out by College Enrollment

Number of Enrolled Students (FTE)	Yes	No
Less than 1,650	44.44%	55.56%
1650 -- 4,000	69.23%	30.77%
Greater than 4,000	50.00%	50.00%

16.11. Percentage of Libraries that Catalog Web Resources, Broken Out by Type of College

Type of College	Yes	No
Community College	57.14%	42.86%
4-Year or Master's Level	45.45%	54.55%
PHD & Research University	66.67%	33.33%

16.12. Percentage of Libraries that Catalog Web Resources, Broken Out by Public or Private Status of the College

Public or Private Status	Yes	No
Public College	46.67%	53.33%
Private College	57.69%	42.31%

16.13. Percentage of Libraries that Make Archival and Manuscript Finding Aids Available on the Web

	Yes	No
All Libraries	31.71%	68.29%

16.14. Percentage of Libraries that Make Archival and Manuscript Finding Aids Available on the Web, Broken Out by College Enrollment

Number of Enrolled Students (FTE)	Yes	No
Less than 1,650	22.22%	77.78%
1650 -- 4,000	38.46%	61.54%
Greater than 4,000	40.00%	60.00%

16.15. Percentage of Libraries that Make Archival and Manuscript Finding Aids Available on the Web, Broken Out by Type of College

Type of College	Yes	No
Community College	0.00%	100.00%
4-Year or Master's Level	36.36%	63.64%
PHD & Research University	41.67%	58.33%

16.16. Percentage of Libraries that Make Archival and Manuscript Finding Aids Available on the Web, Broken Out by Public or Private Status of the College

Public or Private Status	Yes	No
Public College	21.43%	78.57%
Private College	37.04%	62.96%

16.17. Trends in Demand for Librarians Services as a Result of Making Finding Aids Available on the Web

	Demand for Library Service Has Increased	Demand for Library Service Has Not Increased
All Libraries	39.29%	60.71%

16.18. Trends in Demand for Librarians Services as a Result of Making Finding Aids Available on the Web, Broken Out by College Enrollment

Number of Enrolled Students (FTE)	Demand for Library Service Has Increased	Demand for Library Service Has Not Increased
Less than 1,650	40.00%	60.00%
1650 -- 4,000	27.27%	72.73%
Greater than 4,000	57.14%	42.86%

16.19. Trends in Demand for Librarians Services as a Result of Making Finding Aids Available on the Web, Broken Out by Type of College

Type of College	Demand for Library Service Has Increased	Demand for Library Service Has Not Increased
Community College	0.00%	100.00%
4-Year or Master's Level	50.00%	50.00%
PHD & Research University	45.45%	54.55%

16.20. Trends in Demand for Librarians Services as a Result of Making Finding Aids Available on the Web, Broken Out by Public or Private Status of the College

Public or Private Status	Demand for Library Service Has Increased	Demand for Library Service Has Not Increased
Public College	27.27%	72.73%
Private College	47.06%	52.94%

OTHER REPORTS FROM PRIMARY RESEARCH GROUP INC.

PREVAILING & BEST PRACTICES IN ELECTRONIC AND PRINT SERIALS MANAGEMENT
Price: $80.00   Publication Date: November 2005

This report looks closely at the electronic and print serials procurement and management practices of eleven libraries including: The University of Ohio, Villanova University; the Colorado School of Mines, Carleton College, Northwestern University; Baylor University, Princeton University, the University of Pennsylvania, the University of San Francisco, Embry-Riddle Aeronautical University and the University of Nebraska Medical Center. The report looks at both electronic and print serials and includes discussions of the following issues: selection and management of serials agents, including the negotiation of payment; allocating the serials budget by department; resolving access issues with publishers; use of consortiums in journal licensing; invoice reconciliation and payment; periodicals binding, claims, check in and management; serials department staff size and range of responsibilities; serials management software; use of open access archives and university depositories; policies on gift subscriptions, free trials and academic exchanges of publications; use of electronic serials/catalog linking technology; acquisition of usage statistics; cooperative arrangements with other local libraries and other issues in serials management.

CREATING THE DIGITAL ART LIBRARY
Price: $80.00   Publication Date: October 2005

This special report looks at the efforts of ten leading art libraries and image collections to digitize their holdings. The study reports on the efforts of The National Gallery of Canada, Cornell University's Knight Resource Center, the University of North Carolina, Chapel Hill; the Smithsonian Institution Libraries, The Illinois Institute of Technology, The National Archives and Records Administration, McGill University, Ohio State University, the Cleveland Museum of Art, and the joint effort of Harvard, Princeton, The University of California, San Diego, the University of Minnesota and others to develop a union catalog for cultural objects.

Among the issues covered: cost of outsourcing, cost of in-house conversions, the future of 35 mm slides and related equipment, use of ARTstor and other commercial services, ease of interlibrary loan in images and the creation of a union catalog, prioritizing holdings for digitization, relationship of art libraries to departmental image collections, marketing image collections, range of end users of image collections, determining levels of access to the collection, digitization and distribution of backup materials on artists lives and times, equipment selection, copyright, and other issues in the creation and maintenance of digital art libraries.

**TRENDS IN THE MANAGEMENT OF LIBRARY SPECIAL COLLECTIONS IN
FILM AND PHOTOGRAPHY
Price: $80.00   Publication Date: October 2005**

This special report looks at the management and development of America's thriving special collections in film and photography. The report profiles the following collections: The University of Louisville, the Photographic Archives; the University of Utah's Multimedia Collection; The American Institute of Physics' Emilio Segre Visual Archives; The Newsfilm Library at the University of South Carolina; The University of California, Berkeley Pacific Film Archive; the UCLA Film and Television Archive, the Vanderbilt University Television News Archive; The National Archives and Records Administration's Special Media Preservation Laboratory; the University of Washington's Digital Initiatives.

The report covers digitization of photographs and film, special collection marketing, collection procurement, funding and financing, approaches for optimizing both sales revenues and educational uses, development of web-based sale and distribution systems for photography and film, systems to assure copyright compliance, the development of online searchable databases, and many other aspects of film and photography special collection management.

**EMERGING BEST PRACTICES IN LEGAL RECORDS MANAGEMENT
Publication Date: March 2006   Price: $295.00**

This special report is based on detailed interviews with records managers, practice management directors and partners in major law firms and other legal offices. Among the organizational participants are: Kaye Scholer, Fulbright & Jawarski, Kilpatrick Stockton, Thomas Cooley Law School , the National Archives & Records Administration, Thompson Hine, Dewey Ballantine and Blackwell Sanders Peper Martin.

Among the issues covered in detail: Records Department Staff Size, Budget & Range of Responsibilities, Breakdown of Employee Time Use, Space Benchmarks for Off-site storage, Classification Scheme and Planning for Records Retrieval, Integration of Records with Copyright Information, Emails, Correspondence and other Forms of Legal Information, Types of Knowledge Management Software/Systems Under Consideration, Uses of Records Request Tracking, Strategies for Employee and Attorney Training in Content Control, Use of RFID & Barcoding Technology, Pace & Cost of Records Digitization, Digitization Technology & Storage Options, Records Security & Password Strategy, Relations Among the Library, Docket, Records Department, Information Technology Department and other Units Involved in Content/Knowledge Management and much more.

MAXIMIZING LAW LIBRARY PRODUCTIVITY
ISBN 1-57440-077-0   PRICE: $89.50   Publication Date: March 2006

This report looks closely at a broad range of management practices of law firm libraries including those from the following institutions: Foley & Hoag; Northwestern Mutual Insurance; Nelson, Mullins Riley And Scarborough; Cornell University Law School; Schwabe Williamson & Wyatt; Mayer, Brown, Rowe & Maw; Loyola University Law School; Sonnenschein Nath & Rosenthal; Brinks, Hofer, Gilson & Lione; The Civil Court of the City of New York; Beuf Gilbert and others.

The many issues covered include: trends in the physical space allocated to the library, print vs. electronic information spending, retention policies on print reporters, uses of blogs, personnel and training policies, outsourcing, relations with records and knowledge/content management, ways to serve multiple offices and locations, use of RSS feeds and weblogs, uses of intranets and other shared workspaces, information literacy training, favored databases, optimizing librarian time management, management of the flow of reference requests, software selection and other issues impacting the performance of law libraries.

LAW LIBRARY BENCHMARKS, 2004-05 EDITION
Publication Date: August 20004
Price: $115.00   ISBN #: 1-57440-070-3

Law Library Benchmarks presents data from more than 70 law libraries, including those of major law firms, law schools, government agencies and courthouses. Data is broken out by type of law library. Includes detailed data on: library dimensions and physical and "e-traffic" to the library, trends in library staff size, salaries and budget, precise statistics on use of librarian time, spending trends in the library content budget, spending on specific types of legal information such as state and local codes or legal journals, spending on databases and commercial online services, use of and plans for CD-ROM, parent organization management's view of the future of the law library, assessment of library resources for analyzing the business side of law, assessment of attorney search skills, trends in use of reference materials and much more.

CREATING THE DIGITAL LAW LIBRARY
Price: $95.00 Publication Date: June 1   2003

This report profiles digital library development policies of leading law libraries including those of Thompson Hine, Cassells Brock & Blackwell, Seyfarth Shaw, Ivins Phillips & Barker, Querrey @ Harrow, Lawrence County Law Library, Duke University Law Library, the University of Indiana Law Library, and others.   The report covers policies concerning electronic journals, archiving, e-books, electronic directories, database user training, use of alert service, virtual reference services, negotiating tactics with vendors, electronic documents delivery, librarian time management, web site redevelopment and design and other issues.

BEST PRACTICES OF ACADEMIC LIBRARY INFORMATION TECHNOLOGY DIRECTORS
Price: $75.00   Publication Date: February 25, 2005   ISBN: 1-57440-072-X

This study is based on interviews with IT directors and assistant directors of leading college and university libraries and consortiums, including The Research Libraries Group, Vanderbilt University, the University of Texas, Lewis & Clark College, Salt Lake Community College, the University of Washington, the California Institute of Technology, Hutchinson Community College and Australia's Monash University,

Among the many topics covered are: investment in and maintenance of workstations, implementation of wireless access, policies towards laptops in the library, digitizing special collections, establishing digital depositories, preserving scholarly access to potentially temporal digital media, use of Ebooks, services for distance learning students, use of url resolvers, web site development and management, use of virtual reference, investment in library software, IT staff size and staff skill composition, range of IT staff responsibilities, use of outsourcing, relations between Library and general University IT staff, uses of PHP programming, catalog integration with the web, catalog enhancement software and services, web site search engine policies, use of automated electronic collection management software, technology education and training, development of technology centers and information literacy, library printing technology and cost reimbursement, and other issues of concern to library information technology staff directors.

THE MARKETING OF HISTORIC SITES, MUSEUMS, EXHIBITS AND ARCHIVES
Price: $95.00   Publication Date: JUNE 2005

This report looks closely at how history is presented and marketed by organizations such as history museums, libraries, historical societies, and historic sites and monuments. The report profiles the efforts of The Vermont Historical Society, Hook's Historic Drug Store and Pharmacy, The Thomas Jefferson Foundation/Monticello, the Musee Conti Wax Museum of New Orleans, The Bostonian Society, the Dittrick Medical History Center, The Band Museum, the Belmont Mansion, the Kansas State Historical Society, the Computer History Museum, the Atari Virtual Museum, the Museum of American Financial History, the Atlanta History Center and the public libraries of Denver and Evansville. The Study's revealing profiles, based on extensive interviews with executive directors and marketing managers of the institutions cited, provide a deeply detailed look at how history museums, sites, societies and monuments are marketing themselves.

BEST PRACTICES OF PUBLIC LIBRARY INFORMATION TECHNOLOGY DIRECTORS
Price: $65   FEBRUARY 2005
ISBN: 1-57440-073-8

This special report from Primary Research Group is based on exhaustive interviews with information technology directors and other critical staff involved in IT decision-making from the Princeton Public Library, the Minneapolis Public Library, the Boston Public Library, the Seattle Public Library, Cedar Rapids Public Library, San Francisco Public Library, the Denver Public Library, Evansville Public Library and the Santa Monica Public Library. The report – which is in an interview format and presents the views of the institutions cited above as well as Primary Research Group commentary – presents insights into the myriad of technology-related issues confronting today's public librarians, including issues involved with: internet filtering, workstation management and development, PC image roll out, equipment and vendor selection, database licensing, internet-access policies, automated book check-in and check-out systems, cataloging, and catalog enhancement, voice over IP, digitization of special collections, development of technology centers, wireless access, use of e-books, outsourcing, IT-staff training, virtual reference, and much more.

TRAINING COLLEGE STUDENTS IN INFORMATION LITERACY: PROFILES OF HOW COLLEGES TEACH THEIR STUDENTS TO USE ACADEMIC LIBRARIES
PRICE: $69.50   JANUARY   2003
ISBN: 1-57440-059-2

This special report profiles how more than a dozen academic libraries are coping with the surge of web/database education requests. The report covers the development of online tutorials, distribution of teaching loads and levels of specialization among library staff, the perils of teaching library science to English 101 and Psychology 101 students, as well as advanced personalized tutorials for PhD candidates and professors. Among the specialized topics covered: How libraries are reaching out and teaching distance learners and how are they negotiating help from other college departments, such as academic computing and education, and from in-house instructional technology programmers. Other issues explored include the library-education efforts of consortiums and partnerships, use of knowledge-management and reference software for library training, the development of savvy library web pages and tutorials for training, and the thorny issue of negotiating training support from vendors.

CREATING THE VIRTUAL REFERENCE SERVICE
PRICE: $85.00   JANUARY 2003
ISBN: 1-57440-058-4

This report profiles the efforts of 15 academic, special, and public libraries to develop digital reference services. The aim of the study is to enable other libraries to benefit from their experience in deciding whether, and how, to develop a digital-reference service, how much time, money and other resources to spend on it, how to plan it, institute it and evaluate it. Let librarians – in their own words – tell you about their experiences with digital reference.

Among the libraries and other organizations profiled are: Pennsylvania State University, Syracuse University's Virtual Reference Desk, the Massachusetts Institute of Technology, Palomar College, The Library of Congress, the University of Florida, PA Librarian Live, the Douglas County Public Library, the Cleveland Public Library, Denver Public Library, OCLC, the New England Law Library Consortium, the Internet Public Library, Paradise Valley Community College, Yale University Law School, Oklahoma State University, Tutor.Com and Baruch College.

PRIVATE COLLEGE INFORMATION TECHNOLOGY BENCHMARKS
PRICE: $295   JANUARY 2003
ISBN: 1-57440-060-6

Private College Information Technology Benchmarks presents more than 650 tables and charts exploring the use of information technology by small- and medium-sized private colleges in the United States. The report covers both academic and administrative computing, and breaks out data by enrollment size and level of tuition charged. Sixteen private American colleges contributed data to the report.

LICENSING AND COPYRIGHT MANAGEMENT: BEST PRACTICES OF COLLEGE, SPECIAL, AND RESEARCH LIBRARIES
PRICE: $80   MAY 2004
ISBN: 1-57440-068-1

This report looks closely at the licensing and copyright-management strategies of a sample of leading research, college and special libraries and consortiums and includes interviews with leading experts. The focus is on electronic-database licensing, and includes discussions of the most pressing issues: development of consortiums and group buying initiatives, terms of access, liability for infringement, archiving, training and development, free-trial periods, contract language, contract-management software and time-management issues, acquiring and using usage statistics, elimination of duplication, enhancement of bargaining power, open-access publishing policies, interruption-of-service contingency arrangements, changes in pricing over the life of the contract, interlibrary loan of electronic files, copyright clearance, negotiating tactics, uses of consortiums, and many other issues. The report profiles the emergence of consortiums and group-buying arrangements.

CREATING THE DIGITAL ACADEMIC LIBRARY:
Price: $69.50   JULY 2004
ISBN: 1-57440- 071-1

This report looks closely at the efforts of more than ten major academic libraries to develop their digital assets and deal with problems in the area of librarian time management, database selection, vendor relations, contract negotiation and tracking, electronic-resources funding and marketing, technical development, archival access, open access publishing agit prop, use of e-books, digitization of audio and image collections and other areas of the development of the digital academic library. The report includes profiles of Columbia University School of Medicine, the Health Sciences Complex of the University of Texas, Duke University Law Library, the University of Indiana Law Library, the University of South Carolina, the University of Idaho, and many others.

LIST OF SELECTED PARTICIPANTS

Langsdale Library University Of Balitmore 1420 Maryland Ave. Baltimore, MD 21201
Robert Morris University 6001 University Blvd. Moon Township, PA 15108
Hartford Seminary Library 77 Sherman Street Hartford, CT 06105-2260
Luzerne County Community College 1333 South Prospect Street Nanticoke, PA 18634
Rachel R Savarino Library Trocaire College 360 Choate Avenue Buffalo NY 14220-2094
Spring Hill College 4000 Dauphin Street Mobile, Alabama 36608
Vermilion Community College Library 1900 E. Camp St. Ely, MN 55731
Clara Fritzsche Library Notre Dame College 4545 Collere Road South Euclid, OH 44121
Connors State College Library Route 1, Box 1000 Warner, Oklahoma 74469-9700
Eastern Mennonite University 1200 Park Rd. Harrisonburg, VA 22802-2462
Hood College Beneficial-Hodson Library 401 Rosemont Ave. Frederick, MD 21701
Emerson College Library 120 Boylston Street Boston, Ma 02116
Alumni Library Eastern Arizona College 615 N. Stadium Avenue Thatcher, AZ 85552
Western University Of Health Sciences Harriet K. & Philip Pumerantz Library 309 E. Second
    Street Pomona, CA 91766
Krannert Memorial Library University Of Indianapolis 1400 E. Hanna Avenue Indianapolis, IN
    46227
University Of Colorado Law Library 402 UCB Boulder, CO 80303
Pennsylvania Institute Of Technology Library 800 Manchester Avenue Media, PA 19063-4098
Baker University Library PO Box 65 Baker University Baldwin City, KS 66006
Tri-State University 1 University Avenue Angola, IN 46703
Bellevue University 1000 Galvin Road South Bellevue, NE 68005
Seminole Community College - Sanford/Lake Mary Campus 100 Weldon Blvd Sanford, FL
    32773
Mississippi State University College Of Architecture - Jackson Center Branch 509 E. Capitol St.
    Jackson, MS 39201
Mary Kintz Bevevino Library College Misericordia Dallas, PA 18612
Marymount Manhattan College 221 E. 71st Street New York, NY 10021
Southwest Minnesota State University 1501 State Street Marshall, MN 56258
University Of Akron Libraries Buchtel Commons Akron, OH 44325
College Of Mount St.Joseph 5701 Delhi Road Cincinnati, OH 45233-1671
Heidelberg College 310 East Market Street Tiffin, Ohio 44883
Van Wylen Library Hope College P. O. Box 9012 Holland MI 49422-9012
University Of St. Thomas 2115 Summit Avenue St. Paul, MN 55105
Ouachita Baptist University 410 Ouachita Street Arkadelphia, AR 71998-0001
University Of Missouri - St. Louis 8001 Natural Bridge Road   St. Louis, MO 63121
University Of Idaho Library PO Box 442350 Moscow ID 83844
Columbia International University PO Box 3122 Columbia, SC 29230-3122
Hunter College Libraries City University Of New York - Hunter College 695 Lexington Avenue
New York, NY 10021
Franklin D. Schurz Library Indiana University South Bend P.O. Box 7111 South Bend, IN
    46634
Philadelphia University 4201 Henry Ave Philadelphia Pa 19144
Technical College Of The Lowcountry 921 Ribaut Road Beaufort, SC 29901
Neumann College Library One Neumann Drive Aston, PA 19014

The King's University College 9125 - 50 St. Edmonton, AB Canada T6B 2H3
Univ Of Tx Permain Basin Odessa, TX
Marshall University Libraries 1 John Marshall Drive Huntington, WV 25755-2060
York College Library York College Jamaica Ny 11451
Pfeiffer University PO Box 960 Misenheimer, NC 28109
Occidental College 1600 Campus Road Los Angeles, CA   90041